Best T ...

MW01035920

The Fisherman's Guide to Selling

Reel in the Sale—Hook, Line, and Sinker

JOE DiMISA
Senior Vice-President and Principal, Sibson Consulting

BUSINESS

ADAMS MEDIA
AVON, MASSACHUSETTS

Published by
Adams Media, an F+W Publications Company
57 Littlefield Street, Avon, MA 02322. U.S.A.
www.adamsmedia.com

ISBN 10: 1-59337-746-0
ISBN 13: 978-1-59337-746-5

Printed in Canada.

J I H G F E D C B A

Library of Congress Cataloging-in-Publication Data
is available from the publisher.

This publication is designed to provide accurate and authoritative
information with regard to the subject matter covered. It is sold with
the understanding that the publisher is not engaged in rendering legal,
accounting, or other professional advice. If legal advice or other expert
assistance is required, the services of a competent professional person
should be sought.

—From a *Declaration of Principles* jointly adopted by a
Committee of the American Bar Association and
a Committee of Publishers and Associations

Many of the designations used by manufacturers and sellers to distinguish their product are claimed as trademarks. Where those designations appear in this book and Adams Media was aware of a trademark
claim, the designations have been printed with initial capital letters.

Interior art © iStockphoto / Connie Kryzanowski and Esther Lucini

This book is available at quantity discounts for bulk purchases.
For information, please call 1-800-289-0963.

Contents

Acknowledgments

My special gratitude and regards to the many people that have inspired me over the years. Specifically, I would like to first thank my loving wife, Natalie DiMisa, who always provides balanced, objective feedback on all life and business issues. She is a loving mother of our two sons, William and Andrew, and a devoted wife. Without her guidance, nothing in my life would be possible.

Thanks to Bill Martin, my father-in-law (aka Tarpon Willie) who taught me many lifelong lessons and fishing "tricks." His determination and tenacity inspire me each and every day to work hard and think of others. He has openly shared his fishing spots, techniques and business tips. His faith inspires us all.

From a professional point of view, I would like to acknowledge and give a special thanks to Mari Bernhagen for her help in clarifying my thoughts, words, and writing style. She helped me through the process and asked the tough questions when needed. Without her talented presence, guidance, and editing, this book could not have been written.

I would also like to salute the many people that I have worked with over the years who gave me the inspiration for this book. People such as Mark Donnolo, Kathy Ledford, and Bergin Penhart—all three are such talented people. Their feedback, thoughts, and coaching have influenced parts of this book. And to the many clients and/or organizations that I have worked with over the years: the opportunity to serve you, listen to your challenges, and provide solutions has helped take experiences and turn them into a book that will help others as I have been helped.

Lastly, I would like to offer this book as a tribute to my father, Joseph J. DiMisa, who passed away as I was writing it. He never had a chance to read even a single word of the book, but I know he is smiling down upon me.

Best regards to all!
Joe

Charting the Course

"The only thing that matters is a happy customer."
—*Top seller for three consecutive years*
at a business-to-business telecom company

As a younger man, I spent many a morning fishing with my father-in-law, nicknamed Tarpon Willie, a devoted husband, father, and angler. Tarpon Willie loves to fish for all species, but his favorite is tarpon, a fish common to the warm waters of Tampa Bay. (Hence his nickname.) Before I really understood the sport of fishing, we would head out almost every weekend in pursuit of a catch. After boating a few fish, I usually was ready to head home, satisfied with a couple of "keepers." Tarpon Willie, on the other hand, continued to examine the tide charts, watch the currents, and try new baits. He truly was a master and extremely committed to his task. These traits made him successful in fishing and even more so in business.

Tarpon Willie taught me that the most successful anglers are those who are not satisfied with catching just a few fish. They want to catch their limit every time out and do it over a long period of time. The same is true of salespeople. We all have seen the folks who have one big month or quarter and then fade back into average. Those who are truly successful excel every month, year in and year out.

Admiring my father-in-law's zeal for fishing and sales, I started to build both my fishing and relationship skills, all the while growing more and more passionate about catching more fish and providing the best possible products and services to my customers. It's amazing how quickly this passion and quest for excellence correlates with success. It also is amazing how intoxicating it becomes to continually attempt to build relationships and provide value—especially when clients confirm your abilities by purchasing more.

Now, as an experienced saltwater angler and professional sales management consultant, I see strong parallels between fishing and selling. Whether you are landing a sport fish or closing a big deal, it takes a series of critical steps to maximize your opportunities and increase your chances for success.

The biggest fish, like the most sought-after sales prospects, are the most difficult and exciting to attract. But smaller, more frequent catches, like high-volume transactional sales, are just as important and gratifying. When reeling in fish of any size, the adrenaline rush can be compared to the euphoria of a prospect expressing interest in your product or service and entrusting you to fulfill his or her business needs.

Yet you can't be too confident that a nibble will result in a catch. Rush a prospect, and you may lose your catch, whether it's an impressive trophy fish or a million-dollar account. When the fish does take the bait, however, the mission isn't complete until your quarry has been reeled in, the fishing leader has been touched, and the catch has been released unharmed.

Although the strategies used to catch different types of fish or customers vary, the process is the same. It involves planning, preparation, finding the right spot to fish, using the right bait and gear, "chumming" the water, throwing out some lines, and reeling in the fish (or customers).

In my consulting and sales career, I've been fortunate to observe many large *Fortune* 500 companies. I've seen winning sales techniques that distinguish top-performing sellers from "B" and "C" players. Many of my insights have come from the "ride-along" opportunities I've had to observe sales reps on the job. Even though I've been able to observe top salespeople for so long, I am always amazed that the most successful salespeople (that is, those in the top 5 to 10 percent of the reps in their company) possess similar traits, no matter their industry or the product they're selling. They always want to improve and build stronger and deeper relationships with their customers.

So how do you apply fishing strategies to selling? What makes one fisherman or salesperson more likely to succeed than another? In an increasingly competitive marketplace, how can you get the edge that will help seal the deal and keep you at the pinnacle of the top-performer pyramid?

I hope this book answers these and other questions for you. It doesn't matter if you've never fished before; whether you prefer fly-fishing, saltwater, or freshwater fishing; or whether you're a fisherman or a fisherwoman. The concepts are simple and can be applied easily by anyone in the sales profession—which comprises about 15 percent of the U.S. work force, or an estimated 19 million people! In both fishing and sales, if you plan and are well organized, you will greatly increase your odds of success.

I offer this book as a "how to" guide for busy salespeople who want some hot tips in a hurry. I hope it increases your odds of landing more or bigger sales—and maybe even a couple of fish.

CHAPTER ONE

Identify What You're Trying to Catch

WHO ARE YOU TRYING TO SELL TO?

It's tough to catch tarpon in the winter. It's a warm-water fish, so when the temperature plunges, tarpon move south into deeper waters. You can try for hours, but if the fish aren't feeding—or worse, aren't there— you're wasting your time. The quietest boat, best tackle, or freshest bait will do you no good. As Tarpon Willie, my salty ol' father-in-law, says, "If they ain't biting, they ain't biting." An experienced fisherman, Tarpon Willie knows in winter to set his sights on fish that run and bite in cold water, such as trout, redfish, or bass. As an equally astute businessman, he has long applied his wisdom and skill in sport fishing to the business arena—with stellar results.

> **CAPTAIN'S LOG**
> "Don't go out and say you're going to catch 'a fish.' Instead, name your catch—bass, tuna, snapper, bluefish. The more specific you are, the more you'll eat for dinner."—Tarpon Willie

I remember my first fishing trip with Tarpon Willie. I was determined to catch a great fish. My preference was snook— a sleek gray fish accented down the side with a flashy black strip. An elusive prey, it makes quite a commotion when hooked. I've seen a hooked snook pop its tail at the line and run toward a submerged structure in hopes of breaking free. It's a true sport fish that transcends just the sport alone; it's also a great eating fish. I was so sure of my target, I'd already told my buddies what I was having for dinner.

When I told Tarpon Willie my dinner plans and asked where we could catch a large snook, he had a simple answer—Costa Rica.

With those two words, I learned my first fishing lesson: know what you want to catch, but make sure it's realistic and catchable. Snook at that time of year were out of season. Our boat could have been seized if we'd harvested one. Tarpon Willie knew this; I did not. I learn quickly, though.

Since that early lesson, I've been fishing more or less successfully for fifteen years. In that same time, I've been building my career in sales, sales management, and sales effectiveness consulting. With no offense meant toward my sales customers over the years, I've learned that fish and customers have a lot in common. Just as certain fish are active in different seasons, customers vary their buying patterns throughout the month, the quarter, or the year. A sport fisherman has to know the water, know the fish, and chart a winning strategy. Similarly, to be successful in sales, you must understand the market and the customer, and tailor your sales approach accordingly. Knowing what to catch, when, and how—whether in fishing or in sales—brings home the trophy.

As a sales representative, your goal is to land customers. You'll maximize your chances when you do your homework and are fully prepared. That means finding out everything you can about the customers' business: what they're buying, when they're buying, what their fiscal year is, who has buying authority. You have to know your customers better than they know themselves.

THIS AIN'T NO FISH TALE!

One of my recent client engagements involved studying productivity levels of direct sales reps for a *Fortune 500* company. We found that average performers stuffed their nets with unqualified prospects and then couldn't find adequate time for any of them. They lost more sales than they won. Low performers didn't spend enough time qualifying or closing. They squandered time in administrative tasks that could have been delegated or skipped. In contrast, the top 10 percent of highest performers and highest earners did a better job of identifying their prime targets and plotting effective ways to reach them. These reps spent little time with unqualified prospects. Instead, they used their time effectively. When they had the right prospect on the line, they devoted time and energy to tailor their sales approach to meet the prospect's needs.

Learn from Top Performers

In sales, acquiring a base of knowledge about your customer involves "identifying" and "qualifying" those customers. Identifying and qualifying are the first two steps in the sales process (see The Five Steps in the Sales Process Tackle Box) and, possibly, the most important. So how can you apply the top performers' strategy to qualify your catch? Follow these steps:

1. *Scope out the customers for your products or services.* You've got to have a firm handle on the sales potential for your product or offer.

2. *Gain leverage by grouping accounts by common characteristics*—type, size, style, issues, needs, and so on. This will enable you to identify commonalities and, ultimately, speed up your sales process. You can apply your understanding of customers across the group and focus on providing value to your customers.

3. *Qualify each prospect,* making sure you have the right "BAIT" (more on that later) to make a sale.

4. *Focus your approach.* Different accounts require different strategies. You want to apply the best strategy to get the sale.

Scope Out Your Customers

How well do you know your customers? Lack the knowledge, and you'll likely miss the sale. Just as a successful fisherman knows the waters and knows the fish, top sales reps consistently seek out information about their customers to bolster their ability to make the sale. The more you know about your prospects, the better you can make the case for your product or service, showing the customers how it meets their needs.

This is less about marketing and more about gathering all the correct customer information before making contact or responding to a request. Your marketing organization usually will furnish a wealth of information about prospects. Your job is to boil that down into tactical knowledge about each account. Make sure you understand an account's basic needs or the current situation the customer is experiencing.

Gathering this information can be as easy as searching the Web or making a few phone calls:

Review the customer's Web site prior to contact. Look at press releases, management structure, "about us" links, and product and service offerings. A company's Web site can give you a good idea of its history and where it is headed. Don't stop there; go to competitors' Web sites too. Find out if the competitors are doing something your prospect is not. Use this information in your conversations.

Assemble company collateral. It can be relatively easy to gather product information, brochures, and marketing materials about a company. If it's not easily available, ask for it. Most

 Tackle Box

THE FIVE STEPS IN THE SALES PROCESS

1. **Identify** who your potential customers are and why they might want to buy your products or services. This step is about "targeting" your prospects.

2. **Qualify** your identified customers—determine whether they need your product or service and whether that need is worth pursuing.

3. **Propose** your solution to your qualified customers. You may submit a proposal in writing or present it in a meeting, explaining how your product or service will help the customer. Once you reach the proposal stage, your odds of making the catch greatly increase.

4. **Close** the sale by negotiating the final details and terms of the deal. This is the confirmation step, which all reps hope to reach.

5. **Fulfill** your commitment and continue to add value for your customer as you and your company deliver your solution. Don't hand off fulfillment until you know your sale is safe. Stay involved at a high level to make sure customer needs are being met. If this step is botched, so is your reputation and any hope of future sales.

Want to learn more about the sales process? Chapter 7 includes tips on how to best execute each step.

companies furnish this material willingly and promptly. If you don't want to tip off the company about your research, call another division and ask an administrative assistant to send you the material.

Talk to customer alumni. Depending upon your prospect's size, the company alumni network may be quite strong. Former employees can provide great detail about how an organization thinks and acts. If former employees are not available, talk to customers or even current employees. Be open about the kind of information you're seeking and the reason for your pursuit. Your objective is to match your product to the company's needs.

Search the Web for any interesting stories or valuable market information. You'll be amazed at what you can find and piece together. A thorough search can give you a broader perspective of the company and alert you to newsworthy events that may have occurred over the last few years related to the company and industry. This type of search might turn up things that are not openly posted on a company Web site. Being up-to-date on the facts can help you avoid missteps during the client presentation and, in the best case, better position you as prepared and knowledgeable.

 **Catch of the Day**

Customers love competitive information, even if it's all publicly available data. So find it, learn it, and use it!

Group Accounts for Leverage

Have you ever been on a chartered fishing boat? If you have, you'll recall that the captain typically asks the guests what type of fish they want to catch. Based on the answers, he'll supply different tackle and strategies. He'll put weights on some poles to ensure they stay at the bottom to attract bottom fish. He may use bobbers to keep the bait on the surface to catch the surface fish. He may use live bait for some fish, dead bait for others, and even lures for another. Yet, while he employs different approaches, he maximizes those strategies to catch as many fish as possible. He won't set you up with tackle that only attracts bluefish if several types of fish are running that day. The captain's goal is to satisfy your desires and make you look good so you'll go ashore happy with something to serve for dinner, and, ultimately, will book his boat for another day.

Effective salespeople use the same strategies as that boat captain: they apply their strategic information to as many accounts as possible, leveraging their knowledge, skill, and expertise to broaden their sales opportunities.

As you discover more about your prospects, you often can apply information acquired about one or more customers to a broader array of accounts. Basically, you are drawing parallels to help you leverage your recourses and time with similar messages. For this reason, it's helpful to group accounts by similar characteristics. You might group by industry (separating automotive, telecom, pharmaceutical, high-tech, software, and so on) or focus on certain business traits, such as size, location, or revenue potential.

The groupings will help you spot issues or trends among similar customers or industries, and create messages customized for each group. All the while, you're building your expertise, your credibility, and your sales effectiveness. This information can prove invaluable as you plan your sales approach. It enables you to emphasize the prospect's situation rather than your product or service. Demonstrating

CAPTAIN'S LOG
*Heed the advice of
Tarpon Willie: "Know-
ing your fish is catching
your fish." When you're
an expert only in your
own product or offer,
you miss opportunities
to enlighten customers
about their industry,
their competitors, their
market. Better to work
from a broader base
of information so you
can educate your cus-
tomers and converse
instead of "sell." You'll
stand a better chance
of making the sale.*

command of your customers' issues will underscore the value of your product.

Knowing the market also makes your organization look bigger, stronger, and more dedicated to a market segment or industry. An organization that segments its markets and customers appears to have so much business or to be so large that it needs to organize its expertise into different areas. Segmentation also tells prospects that you are so committed to their segment that you have dedicated teams to work with them. The reality may be that a handful of knowledgeable sales reps cover all segments, but the impression provided is of specialized understanding and commitment to a given market.

Do You Sell from a Broad Base or an Issue Base?

Do you offer your customers a broad base of knowledge, or do you focus more narrowly on a single industry or issue? Would a broader focus widen your sales opportunities? Answer the following questions, and then decide.

1. Is your offer or product your main focus and your first approach to the customer? (Answer "Yes" or "No.")

2. Do you open your conversations by exploring and offering information about your clients' position in the industry or their focus on the market? (Answer "Yes" or "No.")

3. Do you have a specific industry insight or perspective rather than a general idea of many issues? (Answer "Yes" for specific insight; "No" if your expertise is in general issues.)

4. Do you focus on a few industries or markets and know the key issues and trends of that industry or market? (Answer "Yes" if you focus on a few industries/markets; "No" if you are more of a generalist.)

If you answered "Yes" to three out of four questions, you are considered an issue-based specialist. You effectively group accounts and gain leverage. As an issue-based sales consultant, you'll close more accounts than a generalist will.

The Big Don't!

While I am an advocate of acquiring a strong and specific base of knowledge, I am not suggesting that you position yourself as an expert when you are not. Do so and you'll get

THIS AIN'T NO FISH TALE!

When I was buying a house in Tampa, I only was interested in one neighborhood. So when I interviewed realtors, I wanted to make sure they knew that neighborhood well. The first realtor assured me that he knew all of Tampa inside and out and would find my dream house. The second realtor sold himself as a specialist in the neighborhood I wanted. He provided facts and figures about the rate of turnover, average selling prices, and even professed to know which houses were about to come on the market. He became my agent. The truth is, he was as much a generalist as the first realtor, but he honed in on my need and leveraged his knowledge to sign me up as his client.

tangled in your own net, as the following war story from the trenches makes clear:

Several years back, a local bank had set its sights on growing regionally. To do so, it needed to upgrade its software to accommodate a larger customer base and more diverse transactions. The bank sent out an RFP (request for proposal) specifying one key requirement for the software vendor: strong banking experience. Responding to the RFP, the account manager of a fledging software vendor inaccurately portrayed his team as "well positioned to meet the needs of the bank due to our *extensive* banking experience."

The RFP won the software vendor a meeting with the bank's head of information technology (IT) and his team. For the first forty-five minutes, the vendor's sales presentation was flawless. The sales team articulated the bank's software needs and smoothly answered all questions posed. Then the client shifted gears. The head of IT asked some pointed, banking-related questions. The sales team exchanged worried glances. They fumbled the questions, trying unsuccessfully to redirect them. Each attempted response made the situation worse, revealing their uniform ignorance of banking, and heightening the client's dismay. Feeling misled, and embarrassed in front of his own team, the client's features tightened into a grimace. His annoyance was palpable. He flipped to a page in the presentation, cleared his throat, and read aloud, his voice leaden with sarcasm, "Extensive banking experience?" Icy silence filled the room. In a last-ditch effort to salvage the sales call, the software account manager took a deep breath, smiled broadly at the client, and commented, "Well, I do have a bank account." The meeting (and, I'm told, the account manager's career) ended right there. Not amused, the client stood, gathered his materials, and walked out without a backward glance.

A week after the debacle, the president of the software firm called the client for some fence mending. The client responded that he had chosen a vendor that had limited banking experience, but was honest. He went on to say that the software sales team would have been better off telling the truth. The lack of candor was the true deal breaker.

Qualify Each Prospect

Fishermen find the fish they're seeking by looking for the right signs, such as birds circling overhead, seaweed lines, a hard bottom, or "nervous" water. When fish are biting, they often move around and strike the surface—sending signals to the fisherman. Potential customers and prospects may do the same. Identifying and spotting the need, interest, and/or buying signs all help guide a seller to a qualified prospect. The right techniques can separate an average salesperson from the extraordinary.

How do you qualify your prospect? Think like a fisherman and get your BAIT—Budget, Authority, Interest, and Timing—ready.

Budget

Too many salespeople spend too much time with prospects who aren't ready to buy or don't have budget permission to make a purchase. To avoid this major time waster, tactfully discover where your prospect is in the budgeting process. The goal is not to figure out how much the company wants to spend (although if a prospect is willing to tell you, don't turn down the information), but to determine whether the money's been allocated or the process is just beginning.

Top-performing reps tell me they start with budget for two reasons: It tells them how quickly a decision will be made, and also whether the prospect is entertaining other sellers. The BAIT Tackle Box in this chapter provides simple questions that will help you sniff out budget issues without offending your prospect.

Authority

How often have you expended time on an expected slam-dunk only to discover that the sale requires two, three, or even four more approvals? Even the best sellers face this dilemma on occasion. If you find yourself in this position frequently, you need to qualify your contacts better. Getting to the right authority isn't always about working the highest level in the organization; it's about finding the person with the proper authorization, and more important, the right knowledge to make a purchase.

THIS AIN'T NO FISH TALE!

Many years ago, I outsourced telemarketing for Bell-South. I held the ultimate authority for buying decisions, but I was young. One vendor obviously thought I was too young to hold any true power. He was bent on meeting my boss's boss. Clearly he wanted to build relationships at higher levels. Yet by trying so hard to climb the hierarchy, he lost the sale he had. I brought in another vendor, who appreciated my position and wanted to build a relationship with me. See the BAIT Tackle Box on pages 14 and 15 for questions that can help you identify your prospects' authority without offending them.

Don't try to penetrate the top of the organization when, at the end of the day, the mid-level executives are actually the buyers. In your haste to get to the top, you may overlook—and in many cases offend—the real buyer.

Interest

To be viewed as a "trusted adviser"—a salesperson who adds value beyond making the sale—and not an aggressive, obtrusive salesperson, ensure that your prospect has an interest or need for your product or service either now or in the near future. Without that interest or need, the best message, process, or technique will fail. In some cases you have to work to find a prospect in need; in other cases, you can help to create a need by potentially unseating another vendor. In both cases, you will be received much more favorably if you determine that the customer has a need and you can fulfill it. The top sellers do this by asking probing questions that match up to the needs they've uncovered. See the BAIT Tackle Box for examples.

CAPTAIN'S LOG

Heed the advice of Tarpon Willie: "Find out what the fish want and give it to them." Use the BAIT strategy to get your client to open up about his or her needs. Then be ready to demonstrate how your product and service can help meet these objectives. Stimulate interest and then lead the client to your problem-solving approach.

Timing

Just as there are fishing seasons, there are buying seasons. Customers may be more interested in your products and services at different points during the year. Maybe their current supplier's contract is up, a new quarter is starting or ending, or they purchase your product during a certain cycle.

To qualify a prospect and assess the account's potential, you need to understand the timing of your sales cycles.

As a consultant, I've had the opportunity to "ride along" with reps on their sales calls. On one such occasion, I was riding with reps who sold print advertising for a large yellow pages company. I observed that the best reps organized and prioritized their accounts in order to maximize their potential and revenue objectives during the finite sales period.

 Tackle Box

BAIT YOUR HOOK WITH THE RIGHT QUESTIONS

Here are some key questions to ask when catching a sale.

Budget: Get a handle on budget issues by asking:

1. Do you need ballpark pricing for your budget process, or do you have an approved budget and need a firm price quickly?

2. How long does your budgeting process take? Where are you in that process?

3. Will the finance department be involved in the process? If so, what are the department's most important issues?

Authority: Find out who the buyer is by asking:

1. Who else needs to be involved in this decision?

2. Is there someone within your organization with whom we should work directly?

3. Are there multiple approval processes that we need to follow?

4. To get a head start on the approval process, should we start working with any other executives?

The reps "laser-focused" on high-potential accounts. They aligned their sales approach with the sales and publishing cycle, and moved in to get the sale. When the selling period was over, they moved on to the next book of business. If an opportunity would arise out of cycle, they only entertained it if they could interest the customer in some other media (for instance, electronic yellow pages) that had an open-ended selling period.

 Tackle Box *(continued)*

Interest: Discover an opening to stimulate interest by asking:

1. What issues is your business facing?
2. What are some things that would make you successful this year?
3. What is the growth projection for the business this year?
4. Are you looking for ways to cut costs?
5. Where do you need to gain efficiencies?

Timing: Clarify the sales cycle by asking:

1. What time of year do you open your procurement process for new partners?
2. When do you begin your budget-setting process for the new year?
3. Are you going to be making a decision on a new partner in the coming weeks or months?
4. Do you anticipate any additional budget at year end, or will it come next year? (This question is less about the budget and more about the timing of when money will be available.)

Focus Your Approach

The best fishermen not only have a clear strategy for the fish they are targeting, they also know why they are targeting that particular species (for example, to catch as many as they can or catch a few whoppers), and where those fish can be found. They know when to run all the way offshore seeking their target fish and when to stay inshore and fish the flats. Selling is similar: Identifying the strategic value of your target will increase the odds of success. Smart sellers focus on real results by clearly segmenting their approach and then narrowing the targets. Skip segmenting, and a seller may as well try to "herd fish."

So what's the value of your catch? Are you fishing for large accounts with a twelve- to eighteen-month sales cycle, or are your sales more transactional (occurring daily, weekly, monthly)? The value of the product and the length of the sales cycle will influence your approach. If you're after a big sale with a long sales cycle, you need to devote significant time to building a relationship, or "wining and dining," as some folks say. Your sales process will involve meeting many people in a company and working all levels of the organization. You'll be networking and politicking more and "selling" less. You also should work more in teams and with your marketing department to ensure that your company and products continually are well positioned.

Tackling the Large Accounts

Casting your net for large accounts takes the patience of a whale hunter, the congeniality of an ol' boy fisherman, the seasoning of an experienced boat captain, and the team orientation of a fishing guide. Keep the following points in mind:

Be patient, like a whale hunter. Big sales don't happen every day; in fact, they may only happen once a year. The key is to work with your contacts and decision-maker to ensure that you are positioned when they do make a decision. Don't push the sales cycle to meet your timeline. Get in sync with your buyer, ease the sale your way, and be ready to spear it when it comes.

Hone your relationship-building skills like a good ol' boy party-boat captain. Salespeople are truly "people who need people." You have to love building long-lasting relationships and truly enjoy meeting new people. This is especially true for selling large accounts. Much as a fisherman studies a navigational chart or tide table, you must stay close and plan a contact schedule to ensure that you are disciplined in your approach.

Think like a seasoned fishing guide. Act more like a strategist or thought leader and less like a salesperson. Large deals in many cases are not sold; they are bought. An organization may only purchase a big item every so often. Therefore, rather than create a need, you must create awareness and position your product favorably. In off-buying cycles, assume the role of a consultant who creates value in order to be well positioned during the buying process.

Support your team like a good crew member. Many large-deal decisions hinge upon the strength of your team. Don't be afraid to introduce others into your account. As Tarpon Willie says, "I've never lost a fish because I had too much help in the boat." Never take the "man in a canoe" approach; always bring your full team and make sure you all work like a team. Don't overload the boat, but make sure each person has an identified role in the process and adds value to the client. (See Chapter 3 for tips on getting the most out of your sales team.)

Sealing the Transactional Deals

To sell smaller or transactional deals, it takes speed, a sense of urgency, flexibility, negotiation skills, and a very tough skin. Here are some strategies to keep in mind:

Emulate the speed of a mackerel fisherman. When selling smaller transactional types of products, you need to be fast and agile. A customer typically makes many of these purchases, and the sales cycle can usually be very quick. If you miss a beat, you miss a sale. It's like catching mackerel during the fall. Mackerel swim in schools and you're liable to get three hits on three different rods. If you're not ready for them, you might lose them all and end up with a tangled mess. Have your product and your pitch down, and be ready to price your offer. If you don't, your competitor will.

Adopt a tournament fisherman's sense of urgency. Greet every day with a sense of urgency and purpose, as if you're fishing in a tourney. As an acquisition specialist, you must seek customers in need, much like an angler chases a school of redfish prior to the tide changing. Be proactive and make every minute of the day count. Whether you are prospecting, qualifying, or providing service to an existing customer, your efforts should focus on reaching your quota and meeting your customers' needs.

Show the flexibility and creativity of a flats fisherman. As a small account seller, you must be able to respond to the customers' changing needs and meet different demands (within reason). A customer who makes many purchases often likes to change things around on occasion. If you're not willing to do that, a competitor will. Variety *is* the spice of life—you may be doing everything right, but at some point the client will inevitably get bored. Do not give the client that chance. Use different approaches; introduce the client to new people; be a trusted adviser. Never take your buyer for granted.

THIS AIN'T NO FISH TALE!

When I worked at BellSouth, the sales organization for the business data division had an aggressive and successful seasoned sales team. Only top people moved into the division, and they made big money. The division head was a veteran salesperson who believed that if a sale was important to a company, the company should stop at nothing to fulfill the client's need and close the deal. She taught the organization to support the sales rep. When an opportunity "came on the line," the whole organization helped make the sale. Reps, sales managers, and the division head attended weekly sales funnel meetings to talk through the risks and strengths of key deals, the competition, and the customers' needs and how we could meet them. Mobilizing the whole team to provide the best value for the customer worked, as the division had the highest close rates in the company. I know some sales reps who superstitiously won't reach out for advice with a sale because they fear bringing too many people into the mix. However, one person in a canoe won't catch a marlin. Teamwork can be crucial, especially for big sales, which demand big thinking.

Hone your negotiation skills like a grouper fisherman. Grouper fishermen have to guide the fish out of the rocks below the surface. Similarly, you must know how to negotiate your prospect through the deal. If you're doing many sales on a consistent basis, most likely your margins (the difference between your cost and the sales price) are smaller. This puts added pressure on your negotiation skills in order not to give away the day's catch. Many young salespeople, excited just to make a sale, lose sight of the terms of the deal. Such myopia affects not only the organization, but also the rep's own pocketbook. Remember, negotiation is a two-way street. It should always be a win-win.

Grow the tough skin of a crusty old seaman. Selling transactional or small accounts gives you many opportunities—and as many wins and losses. Adopt a tough skin, and don't take the loss personally. All people face rejection in life; a good salesperson may face it even more. The key is to learn from rejection and retain your positive attitude.

You need to be creative with ways to keep your customer happy. If your company has developed new products, ask whether your client's company would like to be the testing ground for them. This enables you to get great feedback and exposure for your product or service. It also shows your prospect that you value his or her opinion and perspective.

 ## Catch of the Day

The sales rep who is not afraid of rejection is the rep who tries new things and meets new people. The more opportunities you chase, the more sales you will make. Stay focused on wins, not losses.

What Type of Salesperson Are You?

Do you like to look for new account opportunities and generate revenue quickly for your company, or do you like to build longer-term relationships and sell larger, more strategic deals? In my fifteen-plus years of working with salespeople and sales managers, I have noticed differences in the type of personalities, preferences, and approaches that different salespeople have or employ. In most cases, certain characteristics help define a preference or skill a certain person has for either a quick, more frequent transactional sale or a larger, more strategic relationship sale. What preference do you have? Answer the following questions to find out.

1. Do you prefer the immediate gratification that comes from your sales efforts?
   a. Yes, I get gratification from quickly meeting a customer's needs and then being rewarded for it. **BLUE**
   b. Yes, but I also get gratification knowing that I have explored all avenues with my customers, and they are happy. **GREEN**
   c. I enjoy the art of the sale and the rewards that come with a solid sales process. **YELLOW**
   d. My greatest reward comes after a long sales process that ends in a sale and a satisfied customer. **WHITE**

2. Do you like to build relationships with your clients?
   a. Yes, typically my clients are my friends. **WHITE**
   b. Yes, in order to sell products, it helps to get to know your clients. **GREEN**
   c. Selling is all about building relationships. **YELLOW**
   d. A relationship comes from selling quality products at competitive prices. **BLUE**

3. Do you work at a fast pace, "making things happen"?
   a. Absolutely. As sellers we should always make things happen. **WHITE**
   b. Yes, you should ideally always be moving closer to a close. **YELLOW**
   c. "Making things happen" works at its own pace. **GREEN**
   d. I prefer to let customers determine when things should happen based upon their needs. **BLUE**

4. Do you prefer to focus on your product's value, or your customer's need?

   a. Product value. YELLOW

   b. Customer need. GREEN

5. Do you like to have total control over the sale such that no one else is involved and you make the decisions?

   a. Yes, I prefer to negotiate the terms and navigate the sales process. WHITE

   b. No, I prefer interaction from others. BLUE

6. Do you like working with teams of sellers?

   a. Yes, the more folks involved, the better the deal to the customer. GREEN

   b. No, prefer to have the pressure of winning or failing fall on my shoulders. YELLOW

7. Do you like to engage in non-selling activities for your organization?

   a. Yes, I like to be involved in anything that relates to my sale. BLUE

   b. No, I like pure sales process activities. YELLOW

   c. Yes, if it moves the sale forward. GREEN

   d. No, as a seller, I prefer to offload those activities to marketing or support and focus on the deal. WHITE

8. Do you prefer working with a customer who has a high acceptance of your product?

   a. No, if a customer has a high acceptance already, then he or she might not understand all we can do for the company. BLUE

   b. No, I prefer to work with a customer and gradually show that company the value of my product. GREEN

    c. Yes, then I can go ahead and just work on the finer points of the sale. **YELLOW**

    d. Not necessarily; I like a customer who has an open mind and can come to acceptance quickly once he or she hears all the facts. **WHITE**

9. Do you prefer having a few dedicated clients?

    a. No, I like a lot of clients with many "lines in the water." **WHITE**

    b. Not necessarily; I like a lot of opportunity with prospects and clients. **YELLOW**

    c. Yes, I like to focus on specific clients. **GREEN**

    d. Yes, the larger and fewer, the better. It also helps me to understand their issues and needs. **BLUE**

10. Do you look for new business opportunities?

    a. Yes, I prefer looking for new prospects. **WHITE**

    b. Yes, I prefer looking for new customers. **YELLOW**

    c. Yes, I prefer looking for new opportunities. **GREEN**

    d. Yes, I prefer looking for new opportunities and existing customers. **BLUE**

Let's see where your skills and preferences match up:

If you have mostly **BLUES** and **GREENS** (at least seven to ten total) with Blue dominant, you're a:

Relationship Manager. You are a dedicated and seasoned account manager. You work well with others and have many long-term relationships. You prefer a position that is responsible for selling the organization's products or services and maintaining relationships with a small number of large, named accounts. You like to add value and sell in a consultative manner. You like a position that manages sales activities for assigned, national, named accounts, rather than an assigned territory. You like a position that allows you to coordinate all activities into an account. You have good leadership abilities and enjoy mentoring other salespeople.

Mostly **GREENS** and **BLUES** (five to seven total) with Green dominant means you should think of yourself as a:

Dedicated Account Manager. You are trusted and skilled. You prefer a field sales job that sells the entire product line to multiple assigned accounts. You prefer a "farmer" position, which focuses on retaining and penetrating existing accounts. You are at your best when you have account assignments that include some of the largest, most complex, and strategically important accounts. You prefer a job with responsibilities that include (1) establishing and building relationships with a targeted number of customers; (2) understanding customers' business and product requirements, and leveraging product specialists to develop and present solutions; and (3) account management, including planning and sales forecasting.

If you have mostly **YELLOWS** and **WHITES** (five to seven total) with Yellow dominant, your strong suit is:

Account Executive. You prefer selling to new customers and developing these new accounts. You like the thrill of offering new products and services. You are a dedicated employee and can move quickly around shifting customer needs. You enjoy meeting new people and maintaining ties to an account. You prefer to have short timelines and like the pressure of revenue generation. Your preferred responsibilities include (1) establishing and building relationships with a large number of customers in order to attain sales volume objectives; (2) understanding customers' business and product requirements; and (3) sales planning and sales forecasting.

Mostly **WHITES** and **YELLOWS** (seven to ten total) with White dominant means you should think of yourself as a:

New Business Specialist. You are a "hunter." You love selling a larger amount of products and services. You prefer a position that focuses on identifying and converting new customers. You enjoy a quick sales cycle and are at your best when you are moving fast and generating revenue. You are very competitive and love the challenge of negotiation and closing a sale. Your preferred responsibilities include (1) growing the territory through new business and attaining sales volume objectives; and (2) managing the progression of sales opportunities, from identifying the opportunity through closure.

CHAPTER TWO

Select and Present the Right Bait

PRESENT THE RIGHT OFFERING TO MEET YOUR CUSTOMERS' NEEDS

Reinvention is a fisherman's ploy. The most successful anglers continually reinvent the ways they cast, position, or hook the bait. Sometimes changing just one little thing can land a bigger haul.

One morning Tarpon Willie and I were fishing for tarpon in a deep shipping channel. We anchored up in the shallows and laid our fresh bait right on the break (where the

> **CAPTAIN'S LOG**
> *"Since you can't ask the fish want they want, sometimes you have to figure it out on your own."*—Tarpon Willie

channel gets steep). All signs indicated we were in a good spot. Around us, fish were rolling on the surface and striking the bait before moving through, so we knew the fish were there and feeding. Yet, we couldn't get them to bite. We repositioned our boat, re-angled our bait, and threw out more chum. Nothing worked. Ten more frustrating minutes passed. Suddenly Tarpon Willie exclaimed, "These fish are window-shopping; let's get 'em to buy!" He threw a net into the water and scooped up some skipjack—a smaller, bony, and generally less desirable bait than the ones we were using. "Since the skipjack are here along with the tarpon, they may be the tarpon's plate du jour. Let's see if they'll take this entrée!" With that, he put a skipjack on the hook and threw it into the water. Within five minutes, we jumped a tarpon. Clearly, the right bait makes a difference.

As we learned that day, fish can be choosy. Skilled fishermen quickly learn to check and change live bait often to keep it fresh and looking good. They also know that if fish aren't hitting the lure or the bait, then it's time to try a different approach. If it works in fishing, why not in selling?

As a sales rep, you may need to present your product in different ways before your prospect is inclined to nibble. If one approach isn't working, tailor the pitch or presentation just a degree or two to get results. Great sales reps know their

THIS AIN'T NO FISH TALE!

I once went on a ride-along with some high-tech business-to-business sales reps. I watched the high performers learn from rejection and use the experience to fuel future sales. The top reps employed flexible tactics; they made every sales presentation different. In contrast, low-performing reps consistently presented opportunities to customers in the same way. Win or lose, they didn't change their approach. The "A" reps probably faced the same amount of rejection, but each time, they took something from it. They "re-engineered" rejection so it wasn't a disappointment, but rather a learning experience. They continually enhanced and rearranged their sales pitches to explain the product differently and get the account. They weren't afraid to re-sell a customer to turn a "no sale" into a closed sale.

product or service inside out. They're never caught off guard by initial hesitancy, lack of interest, or inattention from the buyer. Like the best fishermen, successful sales reps consistently explore new ways to entice their buyers.

Differentiate Your Bait

So how do you start? In Chapter 1, you learned how to identify your catch. Now, you're ready to get them interested. Tarpon Willie doesn't just say he's going to catch tarpon and expect them to jump in the boat. He knows he has to find them and get them excited with the right bait.

What Makes You Different?

When hunting for a targeted fish, a fisherman faces competition for the catch. Yet the other anglers aren't the chief concern; the big worry is the fresh, lively bait that might entice the fish onto another's line. It's the same in sales: A competent bunch of competitors are dangling a lot of attractive bait. How you present yourself and your product is your greatest asset—or threat—to capturing a customer. Ask yourself, "Am I grabbing the customer's attention?" If your answer is "Not really," then figure out creative, innovative approaches tailored to your prospect that will differentiate you and your product.

 Catch of the Day

You can differentiate on price, value, time to deliver, extensive experience with similar work or customers, or strong relationships with people of interest to you and your sale. Figure out what the "difference maker" is for you and your product—and use it to stand out.

Get your bait devoured by following RFP selection tips from top reps. RFPs (requests for proposals) are common in many industries. A company sends out an RFP to inform all potential suppliers that the company is looking to purchase goods or services. RFPs are usually very structured; they request specific items or information about you or your company. Depending on your industry, such a request may actually be referred to by one or more of the following terms: RFI (Request for Information), Bid Sheet, Bid Response Sheet, Suppliers Guide or Questionnaire, Requirements Guide, Product Specification Sheet or Guide, and so on.

Whatever term you use, RFPs and similar requests are highly qualified opportunities and extremely competitive. To land your RFP on the top of the pile, heed the following advice from winning sales reps:

Read the RFP carefully and follow directions. Follow the directions to the finest detail. Send the response on time—being late is the kiss of death. Also, as simple as this seems, if the company asks for hard copies of your response, be sure to send the requested number of copies. Many companies use a team to review the responses. Forcing the customer to make the copies is a time waster for them, and a possible competitive disadvantage for you, because the responses that are "ready for review" will be read first.

Follow the format. Many RFPs ask standard questions and identify the questions and requests by number. In your formal response, always repeat questions exactly as they are stated. In written responses, use the same numbering system. The better you match the prospects' formats, the more customized your response will look.

Ask questions (even if you don't really have any). Before submitting your response, follow up with the prospect and ask some questions about the RFP. Your questions can be simple, but not superficial. For example, get clarification on pricing issues, number of products, and timelines. All of these points show that you are detailed and care about your response. Good questions also increase your prominence and help build a relationship—the prospect already is forming an impression based on the call.

Be the first to submit and the last to present. Top sellers believe the first submission becomes the benchmark for measuring subsequent proposals. They also say that presenting last increases your odds of getting the sale. You can't always control the order of the presentations, but if you can influence the order or at least state your preference, try to grab that final slot. When you're last, your prospect has vetted all other competitors and identified their differences. You can probe and discover all that's on the prospect's mind. You get the best opportunity to answer the company's questions, address its issues, and differentiate yourself. It's your chance to make the kind of lasting impression that can seal the deal.

Provide relevant references and ask those references to call the prospect. Your references can have the greatest impact of any component in your proposal. Just make sure the references are relevant; that is, buyers of similar products. To increase your odds dramatically, ask your references to call your prospect. Fewer than 50 percent of prospects actually call references, so be proactive—think of the impact that a call from a satisfied customer will make!

Highlight your best business stats. Typically, RFPs do not ask about the responding company's financial strength or credibility. Since such information is not requested, many sellers leave it out. Yet simple facts can make a difference. Consider the impact of statements such as these: "We have been in business for forty-five years." "We work with every one of your peers." "We have a robust balance sheet and thirty consecutive quarters of profitability." There used to be an old saying, "You never get fired for hiring IBM." Sometimes buyers don't want to take a risk. In a close, competitive situation, a phrase or two about your best traits can win the deal.

 Catch of the Day

The exactness of your response to the RFP communicates a strong message about how well you will treat and respect your customer during the sales process.

Why Should a Prospect Buy from You?

Do you have a handy answer that rolls off your tongue? You'd better. Rule number one in the successful sales rep rulebook is to be armed with a clear, crisp reason why a prospect should consider you and your product or offer.

In the early stages of a sale, your goal is to persuade the prospect to consider your product or service, not to close the deal. Many inexperienced reps fail to recognize this distinction. They try to answer a simple question about their offer with a strong closing statement that turns the customer off. It's like trying to catch little fish with a big piece of bait. If the fish can't get his mouth around it, he may be scared away.

Take Your Time and Tell the Truth

I recently worked with a client on sales positioning. The sales manager complained that his reps weren't closing deals. As our conversation continued, he mentioned that he wanted his reps to move the customer from a qualified stage to a proposal stage within two weeks of surfacing the opportunity. I asked him what happens if the customer isn't ready. He responded, "We force them to be ready. We subscribe to the *Glengarry Glen Ross* theory . . . ABC—Always Be Closing."

If you're not familiar with this David Mamet play and film, its theme is about closing real estate deals any way possible. Unfortunately, the sales manager I was talking with had the wrong mentality. He was instilling improper selling techniques in his sales team, and those techniques were actually contributing to lost opportunities.

The point is, don't over-engineer a simple question or try to close too quickly. When the customer asks "Why your product?" give a confident answer that focuses on the simple truths. The following are a few examples of good responses:

> **CAPTAIN'S LOG**
>
> Tarpon Willie says: "Never let 'em see you coming. The more noise you make, the more likely you will spook 'em." At this early stage of the sales process, stifle the urge to compare yourself to competitors unless your prospect specifically asks. The prospect is evaluating you, your product, and your professionalism. The goal is to convince that prospect to take the discussion further. Keep it very professional.

- We have a product that is well positioned to your needs.
- We have a great fulfillment and service group that will exceed your expectations.
- We have an experienced team of professionals who will work with you.
- We are very customer focused.

Whatever the truth is, tell it. If possible, provide more than one reason, but no more than three. One looks superficial; four looks insincere.

What's In It for the Customer?

An old fishing buddy used to say, "If you bring home dinner, Mom won't mind if you're late." In selling, it's all about what your product and service can do for the customer—but here I mean your individual customer, not your contact's company. If prospects choose to talk to you, are they better off personally? Will this sale help their career? Get them a bonus? Solve a huge problem? Help them stand out?

When you're planning to offer your bait to customers, ask yourself, "How will their decision to talk with me and buy from me help them personally?" Explore the possible impact.

THIS AIN'T NO FISH TALE!

When I started out in consulting, I was hired for my sales background, and had one clear focus—business development. I made a lot of cold calls, attended many business conferences, and handed out my business card to anyone who would take it. One day, I got a call from a contact I had met at a recent conference. He and I had hit it off. He was as new in his field as I was in mine, and our neophyte status was the basis for a common bond. He was a junior analyst in the sales organization of a mid-size company. His organization needed a benchmarking study of industry trends, but they didn't have much budget. Could I help him out? Normally my firm handled much larger projects, but this was my first sale, and I didn't want to turn it down. More important, the client was desperate for the data, and I really wanted to help him out. My firm took on the project and completed it successfully. In the process, I was introduced to more senior people in my contact's organization. Within a few years, my initial contact was promoted. Each year, the sales organization kept sending projects my way. To this day, the organization is among my largest clients.

If you're certain it will be positive, then bring it to life in your conversations when appropriate.

What's Your Competition?

In business, just as in fishing, there are all forms of competition. Especially today, the competition for a business's budgetary dollars can be extreme. Prospects know they can shop for different prices, quality, and volume. In addition, many rivals are competing for your prospect's time and attention. In some cases, those competitors are going head-to-head with you. In other cases, you are competing against other internal threats. As a salesperson, expect all forms of competitive threats and be prepared to mitigate them as much as possible. Here are some common threats and ways to deal with them:

Other fishermen in the water (similar solution providers). Most novice sales reps focus too much on what "others" are doing and not enough on what they themselves do, or should be doing. The most effective way to compete against other sales reps is to focus on your own approach and product. The keener your focus, the less likely the customer is to seek another vendor. In fact, one of the best approaches is to speak positively about your competitors and their offerings. Never, under any circumstances, badmouth or put down the competition. Disparaging comments almost certainly will backfire. Always maintain focus on your own product. The closest you should come to discussing your competitor is to contrast your product with theirs to highlight your product as the better fit for your prospect's needs. Always be very diplomatic in your approach. See the Tactful Ways Tackle Box for suggestions on how to stand out from the crowd.

Too much bait in the water (noise in the market). A common problem for fishermen is the location of their target catch. More often than not, fish gather in a certain area because they're drawn by the natural bait in the water—the smaller fish they feed on. Tarpon Willie says, "Where there's baitfish,

 Tackle Box

TACTFUL WAYS TO DISTINGUISH YOURSELF FROM YOUR COMPETITORS

1. **Ask your prospects** if they are hearing similar things (about price, value, quality, timing, and so on) from others with whom they are speaking. If you're competing against an incumbent supplier, ask how your offer compares.

2. **Highlight your items** that will compare most favorably to your competition. Just make sure you have a good handle on your competitor's position and their product or service. For example, if the competitor only delivers once a week, it may spark some interest if you tactfully point out that your company will deliver three times a week.

3. **Ask your prospects** to list the key things they want from a partner that they're not getting today. If you know your company can meet those needs, confirm your ability to do so. Such responsiveness will hit home. However, if you don't know whether your company can match their demands, don't make any promises. Instead, say you will follow up with others on their request to see how your company can fulfill it. Clients appreciate the need to confer with others to get the best answer, and will lose interest when they feel you're trying to fast-talk them.

there's catchin' fish." The problem is, the "catchin' fish" have a lot to choose from. In sales we call this problem "noise in the market," meaning too many people are trying to sell too many products. The proliferation of products can confuse a customer, who then buys whatever seems like a good deal. The term in fishing is a "feeding frenzy."

There are two strategies when this noise or frenzy occurs: (1) throw everything you've got out there and see what happens, or (2) move to another spot. Depending on your product and the type of seller you are, either approach can work. If you're selling a commodity (a common product that is most often differentiated by price), throw whatever you have at the opportunity. That means people, presentations, sales pitches, offers, and anything else that's relevant. With all that bait in the water, you're likely to get a hit. However, if your offer is more relationship-based and you differentiate on quality and value, then you should move to another spot.

> **CAPTAIN'S LOG**
> Tarpon Willie says, "If you're on my boat, you're my fishing buddy!" Never call yourself or your company a "supplier" or refer to your customer as your "buyer." Use the term "partner." It sends the message that you are committed to trust, loyalty, flexibility, and building long-term relationships.

Bigger-fish food chain (internal politics that can cannibalize your opportunity). Tarpon Willie likes to say, "Sometimes you just can't control what you can't control." Whether it's the wind, the tides, the water temperature, or other fish that eat your hoped-for catch, experienced anglers realize that the fishing is better on some days than on others. The case about corporate politics and internal maneuvering can be easily made. Almost every top salesperson has lost deals due to internal divisiveness. It is by far the most feared competitor, simply because you can do little to overcome it. In many cases, you can't even see it. Just as a shark lurks below the surface and waits to attack an angler's hooked and struggling fish, an unknown insider can come in and kill your deal at any moment for reasons beyond your control. The best way to combat this competitor is to make friends with as many people as possible and continually be on guard for any encroachments against your buyer.

Perfect Your Sales Pitch

So you've figured out what makes you different; now it's time to make your opening pitch. The old-pro fisherman knows how to throw the net in a full circle, rather than a half-moon, to catch more fish. A half-moon encompasses a narrower range. In sales, a half-moon is a lost opportunity, like a sales call without a creative sales pitch. A pitch must be well defined and compelling to attract the buyer's attention.

Reps who maximize their exposure and create excitement always find someone who will listen to their message. It takes a well-rehearsed and compelling sales pitch. We call this the thirty-second "elevator pitch." An elevator pitch is a persuasive sound bite aimed at enticing customers to buy, or at least to let you pitch them further, before the elevator stops and they walk out the door.

Perfecting this pitch is paramount. You want to be able to state easily, crisply, and convincingly what you and your company bring to customers. The trick with this pitch is to make it generic, yet also specific, and concise. In my years of working with world-class sales organizations, I've heard winning pitches, and some real losers. Typically the best elevator pitches emphasize ways in which the rep's company and its offerings improve situations and/or solve problems for the customers. Obviously, if you are heading to the forty-eighth floor, you may be able to say even more. However, you should keep the thirty-second limit somewhat sacred. It's better to keep talking longer if you get the chance than to get cut off before you make your point.

An effective elevator pitch includes the following:

- *Your name, your business, and your experience:* Name of company, size of company, number of years in the business, typical industries or clients you serve.
- *Your impact statement:* "My products help clients to ＿＿ (for example, grow business more profitably, improve their offerings, run their business more effectively).
- *Your product or offer:* "My company develops software that focuses on XYZ." "Our ABC products help to ＿＿." "Our services are geared to increase the client's profitability."
- *Your approach:* "In serving my clients, I am committed to ＿＿(for example, providing the most outstanding service in the industry; providing the lowest-cost product; providing the highest quality).

I heard this pitch given in an elevator and it sure got the customer's attention:

"I work for Express Software. We're a ten-year-old firm that specializes in Human Resource tracking software. Our clients include many of the *Fortune* 500 companies that have a need for more effective solutions to manage their large employee populations. The typical issues and approach are to help clients manage the effective and efficient hiring of new employees. This involves properly communicating the ways in which employees earn all of their compensation rewards, and ensuring that succession planning within companies is managed effectively. As you know, there's a premium being placed on hiring new talent and ultimately keeping this talent within the organization."

Pass the Airport Test

Tarpon Willie assures me that fish, on occasion, will "window-shop" and in some cases track the scent of their prey before striking the bait. A shark, for instance, can smell blood in the water up to a mile away. Once they are close to the target, they may bump, nibble, or circle for a few minutes prior to attacking. Clients do this, too. While they window-shop, they may well be giving you the "airport test."

The airport test poses the question, "Would I want to hang out with this person if I were stuck at the airport for three or four hours?" Making the grade on this test is the most important aspect of the sales process up to this point.

As simple or as shallow as this might sound, you gotta pass the airport test. People like to do business with people they like. I can't tell you how to get people to like you, but I can advise you about the "likeability" characteristics people look for in a "buddy," whether in an airport, a fishing boat, a cramped, crowded office, or an expansive boardroom. The key is to be yourself and practice good neighbor techniques. Tarpon Willie says, "I only go fishing with people I like . . . and I like people who like to fish."

Catch of the Day

How to pass the airport test: Be yourself. Be honest. Listen intently. Be respectful of your prospects' time. Be prepared when you meet with them.

Value Small Victories

Some days the fish just aren't biting. Yet rather than packing it in, it might be a great day to catch bait instead. Catching bait takes considerable skill: You have to look for the "nervous," bubbly water that signals bait below the surface. Then you position the boat and throw the net wide without spooking the bait. It's all about taking it slow and enjoying the process.

In sales, small victories can include handshakes as well as the business cards you've collected, which, when loaded into your database, become the bait to attract sales down the line.

Here are some foolproof bait-building techniques:

- Always get business cards from all contacts you meet.
- Pass around a signup sheet in all your meetings and ask for names, titles, e-mail addresses, and telephone numbers.
- When you attend a conference, ask the coordinator if you can have the attendee list. Most will supply the list of names, with titles.
- In your trade journals, look for all names of interesting potential prospects or industry experts.

In all of the collection approaches, the key is getting all of the information and adding it to your contact lists. You need the discipline to collect them, and even more discipline to record all those contacts into your database. If you're missing a phone number, call the main line of the company in question and ask for the number and e-mail address of your contact. More often than not, if you have a contact's name, the switchboard will give you the rest of the information.

Successful reps savor the small victories such as gathering names and information. They build networks and lay the groundwork, and they have fun while they're at it—it's all part of the hunt!

THIS AIN'T NO FISH TALE!

A large telecom company's business-to-business division benefited from a superior and well-seasoned sales force. Unfortunately, a number of the reps were facing retirement and the company was having a tough time recruiting replacements. Sales in this business were based on relationships; without them, according to conventional wisdom, success wouldn't come your way. Consequently, recruits were hesitant to take the job, fearing they'd fumble when competing against established, tenured reps from other companies who seemed to know everyone in the industry and have contacts in specific companies.

The VP of sales asked my firm to determine what skills could create success in this environment, even if a new hire lacked the experience of a tenured sales rep. We discovered that although relationships were key, many of the most fruitful relations were not built on golf, dinners, or the good-old-boy network. Rather, trust, awareness, responsiveness, and, to use one customer's term, "being present," were the true determinants of success. Many customers said they did business with their main contact not based on a long relationship, but because the contacts were responsive and attentive to their needs. Key rep competencies for this sales organization included providing information, gathering business cards, collecting data, meeting new people, and providing value—all the "little victories" that build credibility.

Details Make the Difference

Competencies are the skills, knowledge, behaviors, and attributes that lead to high sales performance. They constitute the "how" of a sales rep's job. They differ from results in that results are the "what" of your work—the outcomes you achieve by applying your competencies. To say it another way, competencies enable results, and increasingly better results are attained with increased proficiency and more frequent demonstration of competencies.

Bottom line: You don't need to catch a whopper each day, or even know where they are in the water. If you're disciplined and focused on detail each and every day, you can get the big strike, and ultimately, will fish—and sell—like the pros.

CHAPTER THREE

Select and Use the Right Gear

*ASSEMBLE THE RIGHT SALES TEAM AND THE RIGHT
MATERIALS—THEN LOOK AND ACT THE PART*

It's hard to beat a sunny afternoon on the water in Tampa Bay. Tarpon Willie and I were fishing for snapper and grouper at a favorite spot, "cool-wreck," a submerged freighter that had met its fate one stormy night many years ago. I had fished this spot as a youngster, but never with much luck. Even as a kid, I knew the spot had potential but I couldn't figure out a way around its many challenges. Whenever I felt a nibble, the fish would just as quickly try to get free and then snap the line against the jagged edges of the sunken wreck. Ironically, now, years later, cool-wreck had become one of my most productive locations—thanks to Tarpon Willie. "It's all about the right gear," he explained the first time we fished the spot together. "You need longer leaders, less weight, and stronger-test lines to withstand the added friction and pressure on your line." I had always thought lighter tackle would provide the flexibility to reel faster and dodge the wreck. Yet the heavier gear enabled me to pull as

> **CAPTAIN'S LOG**
>
> *"Always be prepared. Keep your gear in good shape and expect the unexpected. Don't lose that 200-pound tarpon because a frayed line snaps."*—Tarpon Willie

hard as I could when a fish struck, and keep my line away from the dangerous old ship down below. It took the right partner and the right gear to turn a years-old challenge into a repeatedly productive opportunity.

In sales, the right partner is your sales team—all the colleagues involved in courting the customer. Your gear is the material you bring on the sales call to demo your product or service. Add in your attire and professional demeanor, and you're prepped with the right stuff to make any sales call a success.

Teamwork Wins the Day

Here's an example of how the right team can make all the difference:

A small, start-up technology firm faced fierce competition from two high-profile competitors in their effort to court a *Fortune* 500 company with a lengthy and cumbersome RFP (request for proposal) process. Knowing it was outmanned, outfinanced, and an awfully small player in a high-stakes game, the technology firm leveraged its best asset—its team. It shuffled the team to give each team member a clear role in the sales process and a "point position" with a counterpart on the customer side. Leading up to the presentation and demo of their product, team members got well acquainted with their prospect. They profiled the company's decision-makers to understand the underlying issues of each. They hunted down data on the prospect's other vendors to discern what made those relationships work—or fail. They analyzed possible roadblocks and determined ways to hurdle them. They even called the prospect's competitors to understand what they valued in their own vendors.

The team sifted together all those different ideas to get a handle on the factors that could ultimately tip the scales in their favor. They concluded that the key to success was communicating effectively and working smoothly with the team of people responsible for product fulfillment and delivery.

When demo-day dawned, the sales team's confidence filled the room. Each team member was thoroughly prepped and well matched with a decision-maker at the purchasing company. Collectively, they handled the presentation and questions posed with the energy and precision of a well-rehearsed play. All of the product- and service-related questions felt familiar and were answered easily. The team's rapport and dialogue was smooth with one another as well as with the prospect. They outperformed their competition and won the deal to unanimous acclaim.

CAPTAIN'S LOG

Tarpon Willie says, "The guy with the biggest boat and the most bait doesn't always catch the most fish." More often, it comes down to who's on the team. Your secret weapon can be leveraging your team to seek the greatest advantage. It's always wise to staff a team based upon the customer's needs, and assign roles according to the opportunity.

Staff a Winning Team

Just as a top fishing guide assembles the right team to work on his boat, a sales rep should form a great team to win and service certain accounts. Successful salespeople know they often can't go it alone—especially in the big deals. So they leverage their support teams, their management, and, sometimes, even satisfied customers to prepare for and close sales.

The sales team can be just as important as the product, and in some cases, the team *is* the product. Let's consider the difference the right team can make.

Common Team Accountabilities

The size of the team and each member's accountability will vary according to the product, the customer, and the criticalness of the sale. Typical roles include the following:

Relationship Builder (Account Manager)

Every team needs a point person who truly understands the prospect's current and future needs, issues, and demands. This is the team's "first responder," the one who takes the customers' calls, coordinates all activities in the account, and leads all phone calls, appointments, meetings, and briefings. In meetings, the relationship builder takes the seat of honor—right next to the customer's main decision-maker.

Senior Presence (Executive Support)

All key strategic or large deals benefit from "gray hair" on their side. A senior company executive will project experience, presence, and confidence; earn respect; and heighten the sales team's and company's credibility. Bring in this individual when the customer involves its own executive decision-makers. Your senior person isn't expected to be conversant in all intimate details of the deal or the customer. Rather, the presence of "gray hair" communicates the importance of the partnership to your firm and assures the customer that its account will be your priority once you win it. Your senior executive should make it clear that he or she has great faith in the account team, follows all account developments, and stays involved via regular feedback with the sales team. Keep the executive working at the right levels of the prospect's organization and outlaw any "jumping" over the main decision-maker to a higher-level leader. Also, don't let this individual usurp accountability for managing the account. Make it clear that the sales team maintains control of the account and that all communications funnel through the account manager. You don't want the client calling your CEO with product questions.

THIS AIN'T NO FISH TALE!

On a ride-along with top reps to see how they manage the sales process, I found a high correlation between top sellers and their proximity to the corporate office. In fact, most of the stellar reps were centrally located within the headquarters (HQ) building. When it came to their sales process, the top reps followed the same steps as the less successful performers. They engaged in the same types of presentations, had the same skills, and used their time in the same ways. Their market potential was similar, as were their opportunities. I decided to probe further by going on some sales calls. When I arrived for my first ride-along, the rep asked if I would mind taking the back seat. I agreed, but asked why. "John is coming along to help close this deal," was his reply. John was the COO.

Turns out one reason the HQ reps were more successful was their access to "mahogany row." They saw the executives every day and had developed great relationships. It was second nature to bring an executive out on a call if a rep thought it would help close a deal. Their presence spoke volumes with the prospects, and the executives loved staying connected to the customers.

Product Expert (Specialist)

Include a technical expert who knows your product or service inside and out. This person will supply knowledge and support and either help you close the deal or work as the main seller when the customer's technical experts are involved. Involve your technical expert in product demonstrations and any detailed product assessments.

Support Person (Fulfillment or Delivery Expert)

After the sale is complete, this team member manages the delivery of your product and service to ensure that the client's needs are met. While good account managers stay involved, their chief task is to develop more business with this or other customers. Consequently, they need to hand over day-to-day management of the delivery details. Give the delivery expert a prominent role in the sales process, especially with a complex sale. In a meeting, he or she should explain the fulfillment details, even citing examples from similar customers if appropriate. The delivery expert's other key role is to form a strong relationship with the customer counterpart who will manage the execution of the deal.

CAPTAIN'S LOG

Tarpon Willie says, "Don't let a deck hand pilot the boat." In a full-team meeting with the customer, never seat the technical expert or support person next to the main decision-maker or in another power seat (a prominent seat at the table). Reserve the power seats for the account manager, executive presence, or industry expert.

Industry Expert (If Not the Account Manager)

Bring in your "secret weapon" to display depth and strength in industry trends and relate the customer's issues to those of competitors and peers. Give this key team member a prominent role in all meetings, and encourage him or her to form strong relationships with the customer.

What Role Can a Customer Play on Your Team?

One of the most impressive and influential members of your sales team may be another satisfied customer. Consider how powerful your sales pitch will be with a delighted customer singing your praises. Customers who attend meetings, write letters, or join via the phone can do all of the things that you, as the seller, are not supposed to do: They can talk about your competitors and their experiences, good or bad, without reservation. They can brag about you without sounding arrogant or pompous. They can ask questions that won't appear to be manipulative or a positioning ploy.

Important note: Before you extend an invitation to a client to accompany you on a sales presentation to a prospect, make sure your prospect will welcome another customer's presence.

How Many People Should You Bring to a Sales Call?

There is no hard-set answer to this question; rather, there are several factors to consider:

How many people will the customer have at the meeting? Take your cue from your customer. If the customer plans on having two of the customer's people in the meeting, you are okay to attend the meeting alone, but you also could bring one other member of your team. If the customer has more than three participants, add one extra person on your side. The key is to not overwhelm them with team members, or underwhelm them by a lack of support. If you don't know the customer's plans, ask about the size of the room and the number of people attending. Make sure you state how many you will bring, and ask for feedback.

THIS AIN'T NO FISH TALE!

Several years ago, I helped a telecom company select a software vendor. After reading the proposals, we narrowed the field to three finalists. As in a derby-day fishing tournament, the finalists had one meeting to prove their merit.

The first two teams gave strong presentations, impressing the selection committee with their command of the issues and the features of their systems. It looked like a tough decision until the third finalist. By prearrangement, this vendor brought a "user" guest. After the introduction, the account manager turned the demo over the guest—an IT software manager of another telecom company who had installed the vendor's software. The selection committee was disgruntled by this repositioning, but kept an open mind. As the guest took the head of the table, she said she was excited to help the software vendor since it had helped her by providing a superior product with excellent support. She demonstrated the system, emphasizing that the product was so user-friendly that she felt comfortable explaining it to a group of strangers even though she had only been using it for five months. She pointed out functionality that was perfect for telecom companies, and used terms in ways that only a telecom company employee would understand. In her summary, she shared her selection criteria, explaining that this vendor had met each standard, hands down.

As she ended the presentation, we were coming out of our chairs. This telecom IT manager, with no sales experience and no vested interest, had effectively conducted the demo, answered the key selection criteria questions, customized the presentation to meet our needs, and shot down the competition. The deal was won! As good as the first two presentations had seemed, they didn't come close to making an impression this powerful.

Who will represent the customer in the meeting? In addition to the meeting head count, confirm the roles and responsibilities of the customer attendees. If a support person is coming to the meeting, you're likely to face support-related questions. Therefore, either be prepared to answer them, or bring someone who can.

What are you going to discuss? Confirm the topics and agenda for the meeting. Never leave the conversation to chance. Even reps comfortable "shooting from the hip" can be caught by surprise by an unexpected question or topic. If the client wants to cover detailed product requirements, always have your specialist available, either in person or by phone.

What are you selling? A complex sale of a multifaceted product or service demands a robust team. The customer will expect to meet, or at least have the contact information of all the key players touching the order.

What impact will your team make? Always strive to make a strong, lasting, positive impact. Just as the telecom IT manager mentioned earlier came in and swept us off our feet, you should try to do the same. The stronger the commitment and dedication demonstrated during the sales process, the more comfort you create for the client as he or she determines whether the company wants to work with you. Introduce team members who will make an impact. Just make sure the impact is positive.

CAPTAIN'S LOG

Tarpon Willie says, "If you're fishing for shark, make sure your guests don't mind seeing a little blood." Bringing customers to sales calls can be a risky proposition. Make sure you know what they're going to say and do. Also, make sure they're politically astute, honest, and trustworthy. The risk is great, but if they truly love your product and can comfortably discuss it, the results are undeniable.

What If Your Only Team Is You?

No problem—if you are the whole team, you get to showcase your knowledge and commitment. Many sales are won through a "lone wolf" type of role. Examples are the "hunter" who does nothing but seek out and pursue new prospects; a call center

 Tackle Box

THE SIX MOST IMPORTANT ROLES IN THE MEETING

For a team to work together, everyone must know the parts they are playing.

1. **Leader**—pilots the meeting or discussion. Note: This is a one-person role. Even in the case of cofacilitators, one person must hold ultimate authority. Work this out in advance of the meeting.

2. **Color commentator**—adds important facts about a key issue or reflects on the conversation at hand.

3. **Note taker**—records terms, agreements, needs, desires, and other important comments and decisions.

4. **Bagman**—brings the materials you need for the sales call, from the presentation copies and collateral to the projector. This person ensures that everything you need for an effective meeting is assembled, accurate, and available. The note taker may assume this role.

5. **Name taker**—gathers business cards and/or passes around a list to record the meeting participants' contact information. May also be the note taker and/or bagman.

6. **Coordinator**—makes sure everyone understands their role and fulfills it. The account manager typically assumes this role, but it can be delegated to an administrative assistant, the note taker, the bagman, or the name taker.

rep who handles customers one by one over the phone; or a rep who sells a simple product that requires very little time or interaction with others. If you are a solo seller, your "team" is your materials, your qualifications, your experience, your communication skills, and your dedication to helping the customer.

Access the Right Materials

Experienced anglers rely on the right gear to catch fish, like extra rods and a tackle box full of hooks, lines, and bait. Before heading out in the boat, they oil their tackle and sharpen their hooks. Of course, the size of the gear must match the size of the fish they're trying to hook. Light tackle and a canoe work for trout fishing, but won't help catch a shark. The shark will bite right through the line. By the same token, heavy tackle is wasted on smaller fish that require a gentler touch, a

THIS AIN'T NO FISH TALE!

A sales organization was assembling a team to close a sale with an established, conservative Southern company. Although the sales team believed they were "this close" to winning the account, they did not want to leave anything to chance. So they brought in their top closer, an aggressive guy with persuasive skills and a track record of driving home sales. The team failed to realize that this customer did not want to be sold. This traditional company had already decided to buy and they anticipated a congenial discussion to sort out final details. The aggressive closer was the wrong team member for this customer—so wrong, in fact, that the team lost the sale.

transparent fishing leader, and a nearly invisible hook. In addition, depending on the day's conditions (sun, wind, or rain) the most experienced fisherman make sure they've packed the proper sun-reflecting gear or rain "slicks." In most cases, once you're out on the water, it's hard to head back to the dock to pick up any overlooked supplies.

Just as the tackle box should always be handy, there are required materials for every sales call. Some of the "material" is knowledge—knowing how to leverage technology and being equipped with a solid grasp of the industry and product trends. Other materials are more basic, such as the client's address, building location, the conference room number, and your contact's name and number. As obvious as this seems, many of my customers tell me that at least half the time, sales reps call twenty minutes before the meeting to ask the address, get directions, or confirm other details. Unfortunately, the message they really send is that they're unprepared.

CAPTAIN'S LOG

Tarpon Willie says, "Always thank the guy who fixes your cast net; he is one important asset." After every sales call, send a note thanking the client for allowing you to listen to company issues and present options to fulfill the client's needs. A thank-you note is a small gesture that can go a long way. It also can differentiate you and demonstrate your thoughtfulness.

Once in the meeting, learn and record the names of your prospect's team. In your materials, strategically place a sheet that asks for names, titles, phone numbers, and e-mail addresses of all meeting participants and/or others who will be involved in your endeavor. This helps you and your team document all meeting attendees, and more important, remember their names and roles. It is also a great way to build your contact database.

Another important item of gear is your business card. Have you ever run out and found yourself staring at a client's outstretched hand with nothing to present? If you have, you made a mistake and risked appearing unprepared in your prospect's eyes. Make sure you bring enough cards to hand out to everyone in the room and anyone else you may meet during your sales call.

Bring your calendar to the sales call. This is becoming easier with the combination of phones and PDAs. Be prepared to lock in a date and time if a customer invites you to return to meet others, or attend another meeting. Having your schedule at your fingertips increases the probability of your getting the meeting date.

Bring enough copies of your collateral and presentation. In addition, if you've prepared a PowerPoint presentation, make sure your customer has the equipment to project it. If not, bring a projector.

Look and Act the Part

A fishing-boat captain may not lay down a dress code, but Mother Nature will. With the wind, sun, rain, or temperatures changing quickly, experienced anglers know to check the weather patterns and conditions before they head out to sea. They stock sunscreen, UV-blocking hats, extra shirts, sunglasses, and a rain jacket.

On a sales call, proper attire and appearance count too. You are a direct reflection on your company. Make sure you always look professional and fit in with the prospect's environment. Understand the client's dress code and match your wardrobe accordingly. Corporate casual or a full suit and tie? Do they wear jeans in the plant, or khakis? Don't make the misstep of showing up in a golf shirt when your client's in pinstripes. Nine times out of ten, if you wear the wrong gear, you'll lose your sale. People like to do business with folks they like, trust, and understand. If you come in wearing something that doesn't fit in, you're demonstrating that you don't understand the company's culture. Consequently, that customer might not want to do business with you.

Here are a few guidelines to keep in mind:

1. If you don't know what to wear to your client's offices, ask. Don't leave it to chance.

2. Take a look at the top-performing reps in your company. Dress in a similar fashion.

3. Follow your own company's dress code. At my former company, the policy was to wear a suit to all first sales calls. After the first meeting, if the client was casual, we could lose the tie and wear a sport coat and button-down shirt.

4. Always keep a few essential clothing items in your car. You never know when that soup at lunch will leave a stain, or a team member might forget his tie.

And here are some tips on how to present yourself in the best light:

Men:
- Keep your hair neatly trimmed.
- Forgo after-shave.
- Avoid open collars on your button-down (first button okay if no tie).
- Wear matching belt and shoes.
- Shine your shoes.
- Keep your shirt tucked in.

- Always wear a sport jacket on the first visit, or a suit if it's a formal meeting.
- Wear a T-shirt under a button-down shirt for a neater look.

Women:
- Do not wear open-toe shoes, slingbacks, or flip-flops.
- Keep makeup natural.
- Wear only conservative jewelry.
- Skip the perfume.
- Make sure your skirt isn't too short or too tight, and watch the cleavage—it's great to look feminine, but not provocative.

 Catch of the Day

Being polished, confident, and prepared is an imperative, whether you achieve it through the right training and coaching or wearing the right clothes.

Speak the Language

A salesperson needs a good vocabulary coupled with an understanding of the impact words can make. Use vocabulary appropriately and exhibit a strong command of the English language. Using the wrong word in a sentence can create a bad impression with your clients or make them feel uncomfortable. Use words that show your maturity and your knowledge or education, and that create a comfortable atmosphere.

To be considered a pro in any field, you have to understand and speak the language. Whether you're a new sales rep or a veteran, knowing the language is crucial to fitting into your sales organization and to understanding your customer.

Let's test your knowledge. When a district manager talks about the pipeline, is this a reference to (a) closed deals, (b) sales opportunities, or (c) current accounts? If you answered "b," you recognize that "sales opportunities" and "pipeline" are synonymous. Both refer to qualified opportunities with the potential to become a sale. If you're still puzzling over the answer, refer to the Glossary on page 221 to acquaint yourself with some common sales terms.

THIS AIN'T NO FISH TALE!

The importance of speaking the language—and making sure that those around you understand the lingo too—was brought home to me when conducting a sales training session attended by new sales reps. I started the discussion around the CCOS the organization had to achieve, the predefined excellence points and thresholds, and how the accelerating commission plan would work. I viewed these as important and emotional topics. I was well into a discussion of the funnel, focusing on the probability of closing deals and the ultimate yield the company could expect, when it registered that too many of the faces in front of me were sending back blank looks. Being new to sales, no one in my audience wanted to admit that the terms I was throwing out so casually might as well be an ancient language. Once I backed up and defined my terms, the blank stares turned into nodding heads and looks of knowledge. The group went on to fulfill its promise, delivering a stellar sales season for the company. It's all about knowing the language.

Sales Vocabulary Quiz: Can You Speak the Language?

Choosing the right word can turn a prospect into a golden opportunity. Select the words that are most appropriate when discussing the sales process with a client.

1. Which is the right word?
  a. Contract
  b. Signature
  c. Paperwork
  d. Agreement

2. Which is the right word?
  a. Close
  b. Sell
  c. Purchase
  d. Select

3. Which is the right word?
  a. Present
  b. Propose
  c. Pitch
  d. Negotiate

4. Which is the right word?
  a. Margin
  b. Commission
  c. Fee
  d. Cut

5. Which is the right word?
  a. Sale
  b. Deal
  c. Transaction
  d. Opportunity

6. Which is the right word?
  a. Total Cost
  b. Total Price
  c. Total Investment
  d. Total Amount

7. Which is the right word?
  a. Meeting
  b. Appointment
  c. Lunch or Dinner
  d. Presentation

CAPTAIN'S LOG
Heed the advice of Tarpon Willie: "You gotta speak the fish's language. Make sure they realize that bait is for them. Tug it or jerk it every couple of minutes so it makes a few sounds . . . but be careful; jerking it too much is akin to talking too much." Never talk over your customer. Avoid acronyms, jargon, or lingo.

Answer Key:

1. **"D" IS CORRECT.** "A" is too formal; "b" is too threatening; "c" sounds like busy work.

2. **"D" IS CORRECT.** "A" sounds concurring; "b" sounds like a hustle; "c" sounds like a client needs to make a decision.

3. **"A" IS CORRECT.** "B" sounds like selling; "c" sounds like you have an angle; "d" signifies a give-and-take.

4. **"A" IS CORRECT.** "B" sounds like you are making money off of the client; "c" sounds like a direct charge; "d" sounds like you took a piece of flesh.

5. **"D" IS CORRECT.** "A" sounds like an event; "b" sounds like a negotiation; "c" sounds impersonal.

6. **"C" IS CORRECT.** "A" sounds like a payment needs to be made; "b" sounds like a cost of the business; "d" sounds too financial.

7. **"C" IS CORRECT.** "A" is too formal; "b" takes up space on a calendar; "d" sounds like a sales pitch.

Now add up your answers:

- Six out of seven right—you're a smooth operator.
- Five out of seven right—you're an experienced seller.
- Three to four out of seven right—you're getting close.
- Fewer than three right—you need to find a mentor to help you work on your verbal communication skills.

CHAPTER FOUR

Use Your Time Wisely to Learn Where the Fish Are Schooling!

DON'T WASTE TIME ON THE NONESSENTIALS

I t was derby day of the Sun Coast Tarpon Roundup—one of Florida's largest fishing tournaments in the late 1980s. All derby qualifiers had caught either three tarpon over an eight-week period or one 125-pounder. Now the grand prize and a year's worth of bragging rights would go to the angler who boated the largest tarpon on this final day. Derby Day marked Tarpon Willie's biggest fishing moment ever. He'd been planning for the day all week. "I've been scouting those tarpon so closely, it's like I'm one of 'em," he told me. "I know where they've been and where

CAPTAIN'S LOG

"The early bird really does get the worm— and the fish. The best fishermen are on the water early, when the sun rises and the fish start to feed . . . and they don't fritter away time on unimportant things"—Tarpon Willie

they're headed. My fishing mates have their eye out for other pods just in case mine scatter. I've studied the tide charts, wind conditions, and water temperatures. And those circling birds will lead me to the shad bait. If I don't bring home the trophy, it's not for lack of planning."

By 5:00 A.M., Tarpon Willie was on the water, anchored up in the spot he'd picked as his best shot. Tournament start time was two hours off, so Tarpon Willie filled the time by cutting bait, chumming, sharpening his hooks, and watching the water. As 7:00 A.M. approached and the sun started to break, he started to see his fish. At precisely 7:01, he threw out his first pole. Within five minutes, he had three more poles in the water. By 7:10, he had his first strike. At 7:35, Tarpon Willie reeled in the biggest fish that would be caught that day—a 142-pound tarpon that also won him a boat, motor, and trailer valued at close to $100,000 in today's dollars.

"In my mind," Tarpon Willie told me, "I caught that fish a week ago. I was so ready for him, I almost willed him into view."

Lesson learned: Plan your day in advance and use your down time to maximize your opportunities. Successful sales reps understand this lesson well; they know that sales happen through time spent on the relationship and attention to details.

Make Your Time Count

Time is a valuable commodity. Unfortunately, many reps struggle to manage it wisely. The nature and flexibility of the sales job heightens the challenge. As a rep, you're probably not tied to an office forty hours a week. You may work from home, or face long hours or days on the road between meetings with no planned or structured activities. Consequently, you don't feel the pressure of "watching eyes" or a fiery sales manager following up on every task or pushing you to be more productive. In fact, most salespeople are left to their own devices and are only held accountable for their final numbers.

Given the lack of structure, it's easy to waste time on nonproductive activities. Yet the number one thing that separates top sellers from their mediocre counterparts is the ability to discipline themselves and use their "down" time to plan or create awareness for themselves and their product.

When faced with unscheduled pockets of time, top performers use that time effectively. They don't waste it; they steel themselves to focus on the task of becoming a better account manager or industry expert. They engage in activities that drive interest in their product or service. They realize that those unclaimed hours between sales calls can be the best time to look for new opportunities, visit an old client, or get to know a potential new one.

 ## Catch of the Day

A secret top sellers share is great time management skills—that's what separates them from lesser performers.

Avoid Common Pitfalls

So why don't all salespeople use their time wisely? Unfortunately, they face some common pitfalls and lame excuses, which ultimately create barriers to their own effectiveness.

Excuse #1: "I need time for me."

Many average performers hold the notion that top sellers are workaholics with no outside interests. Truth be told, top performers generally have more productive, effective, and prosperous lives, from both a personal and professional perspective. They use their time wisely, focusing on activities that will make them better sellers, suppliers, friends, and employees. They have made a conscious decision to allocate their time every day to maximize their results.

Excuse #2: "I only want to close."

Tarpon Willie says, "To go where the fish are, you have to know where they are." Well, to know where they are, you have to put in your time and do all the things that position you to catch them. I've talked with sales reps who hold unrealistic ideas about how to sell. They expect marketing or advertising to hand them the leads. Then their job, they tell me, is to field the leads and make the sale.

Selling is not all about closing deals; selling is a five-step process (see Chapter 7) with closing being just one step. Reps who claim to be "a closer" and only want to spend their time closing probably don't seal as many deals as they'd like you to believe. If you lack understanding of the entire sales process, it's likely that you're squandering time. Closing directly correlates with the time spent up-front doing all the activities that stimulate the sale. The more time you invest in focused activities, such as making phone calls, sending letters, meeting new people, and following up, the more deals you'll close.

Excuse #3: "I'm too busy with this one account; I don't have time to sell to others."

Many reps who work with a just a few customers for long periods become so involved managing the accounts' day-to-day details that they lose track of the need to create more opportunities with that client and with others. Top-performing reps make sure to avoid this trap; they balance their time between managing existing accounts and creating new opportunities with those accounts and new customers.

CAPTAIN'S LOG

Tarpon Willie says, "The fish still in the water are as valuable as the one in the boat." Don't sacrifice the larger picture for just one sale—think bigger than that.

Excuse #4: "I've already met my quota."

Too many reps make a sale, tie up the loose ends, and then figure they've met their objective for the day, the week, or month. They tally up their expected commissions and decide they've earned enough to take some time off. Unfortunately, while they're playing golf with their pals, others reps may be enticing their customers and/or prospects with a new product or service. Reps who kick back and turn off may damage their earnings potential, too. Some compensation plans include an accelerated commission rate for sales over quota. Such a feature can pay out two or three times the basic rate. For top sellers, making quota is only part of the job. They are driven by the desire to continually create new opportunities and be recognized as a sales leader. Plus, they know that beyond quota, the payout can increase exponentially.

Excuse #5: "It takes too long to get paid for this sale."

A sales cycle of three months or more can sap your urgency and drive to perform because it takes so long to close one deal. Because a long sales cycle in turn creates a longer reward cycle, you may ease up on the daily and weekly activities that can help close the sale or bring other sales to the table. I've seen reps turn off the engine and idle for a while because they can't realize an immediate impact from investing time in awareness activities. Consequently, they lose focus—and more important, lose the time. If you want to be successful, keep working. The time you invest has a direct correlation to more sales.

Excuse #6: "This customer has bought from me before."

Rely too much on one customer or one opportunity, and you may miss others. Tarpon Willie never likes to sit in a spot too long if the fish aren't biting; he moves around until he finds a spot that will produce. Learn from his example; don't waste all your bait in one spot just because that spot had been productive before. You surely will neglect or miss other opportunities. Instead, always keep your business development engine in gear, searching out new prospects. If you waste all your time hoping that your old customer is going to produce, you may miss your quota.

 Catch of the Day

Being successful in sales is about working and closing many opportunities and doing it consistently over an extended period of time. Don't just focus on past success.

Track Your Selling Versus Non-Selling Time

Most sales reps will tell you they don't waste time. They put in their forty to fifty hours a week and work hard each and every day. Yet success doesn't equate with hours spent on the job; it's the activities you engage in that count.

What it's about is "working smart" versus filling time. In sales, it is crucial to work smart each and every day. As a rep, many daily activities may not have a clear and immediate short-term payoff in terms of a sale. Yet you need to be incredibly efficient with your time and try to engage only in activities that either will stimulate a new sale or support one you've made.

As a rep, your sales clock registers two types of time: selling time and non-selling time. They are characterized by these activities:

- Selling time is spent on customer contact or general sales planning. Direct customer contact includes face-to-face meetings, entertainment, or telephone conversations.

General selling comprises account planning, developing other business, or resolving customer issues.

- Non-selling time is spent on activities not directly related to customers or prospects. This includes administrative tasks, internal meetings, training, travel, or other non-selling functions that do not involve direct contact or direct support of a customer or prospect.

Clearly, the goal is to spend as much time as possible on direct selling activities, while avoiding or reducing the time spent on non-selling activities.

The following table breaks down the "time clock" of an average sales performer. Such average performers spend only 27 percent of their time on customer contact while forfeiting 40 percent to administration. No wonder they are less productive than top sellers.

THIS AIN'T NO FISH TALE!

A recent productivity study that my firm conducted shows that average-performing sales reps spend only about 35 percent of their time in direct selling but devote a whopping 65 percent to non-selling activities. In contrast, high-performing reps allocate their time much differently—55 percent selling and 45 percent in non-sales activities. Top reps don't wait for leads to fall into their lap; they make sales happen. They spend time creating awareness, which in turn will generate sales. By the end of this chapter, I hope you'll be convinced that spending just 5 percent more time each day on direct contact activities will measurably increase your output of leads, qualified opportunities, and ultimately, closed deals.

Average Performers' Time Clock: 35% Selling; 65% Non-Selling

Customer Contact	27%
Entertainment	4%
Face-to-face meetings	10%
Telephone	10%
Other	3%
Other Selling Activities	8%
Account planning/Awareness creation	2%
Issue resolution	5%
Other business development	1%
Administrative	40%
Checking commission reports	10%
Expense reporting	5%
Internal processing	25%
Internal Meetings	10%
Sales meetings	8%
Company-wide meetings	2%
Training	3%
Travel Time—Non-Selling	10%
Other Non-Selling	2%

In contrast, the "time clock" of a top performer shows an emphasis on direct customer contact. Top performers spend about as much formal meeting time with customers as average performers do, but devote double the time to entertainment and telephone contact. They also spend more time on account planning and awareness activities that stimulate interest in their products or services. Most telling is the 20 percent given over to administration—less than half of their "average" counterparts. Working efficiently and effectively is their priority.

Top Performers' Time Clock: 55% Selling; 45% Non-Selling

Customer Contact	38%
Entertainment	8%
Face-to-face meetings	11%
Telephone	17%
Other	2%
Other Selling Activities	17%
Account planning/Awareness creation	8%
Issue resolution	6%
Other business development	3%
Administrative	20%
Checking commission reports	5%
Expense reporting	5%
Internal processing	10%
Internal Meetings	10%
Sales meetings	8%
Company-wide meetings	2%
Training	3%
Travel time—Non-Selling	10%
Other Non-Selling	2%

Find Ways to Create More Time

Non-selling activities "contaminate" your time. To join the top-performer ranks, you must purge your day, week, and month of as many "contaminants" (non-selling-time activities) as possible. Decontaminate your time: Worry less about internal politics. Turn your back on activities that sap your energy but don't generate revenue. Focus, instead, on revenue-producing actions. Each time you begin a new task, ask yourself this question: "Is this going to help me meet, service, or sell a customer?" If it won't, replace it with activities that will.

Adopt a Personal Planning Process

A personal plan can sharpen your focus on selling time. Plan each day purposefully, so you know what you need to accomplish. The following four steps can help you stay on track and keep your goals in sight:

1. *Identify personal goals* (personal growth, earnings, and so on) that correlate with job success. Be specific about what you personally want to accomplish in your job. Establish time commitments (for example, I will invest X number of hours each week). Identify specific objectives around the accounts (for instance, I want to generate X amount of revenue from ABC account), and then detail the activities that you will accomplish to make those goals happen. Be sure to establish objectives for customer retention, penetration of existing accounts, and/or new account acquisition.

2. *Understand your territory and ensure that your personal goals track with your sales quota and other sales accountabilities.* If your goals don't align with your job expectations, realign them as appropriate to position yourself for success. For example, start with the results you must accomplish. Break those down into daily goals. Then identify the specific activities required to meet these daily goals. If your activities won't get you to the required results, realign them until they do. For example, if you want to generate $1,000 a day, every day of the week, make sure that the target gets you to your monthly quota. Or if you want to generate $20,000 in commissions by the end of the operating period, determine how many sales you have to generate on a daily basis. Then see if that goal aligns with your accounts and daily commitments.

3. *Commit time to each step in the sales process* for each week, month, and quarter. Allocate time to fishing for new business and servicing existing customers. You should also determine "stretch" goals that would make you a top earner.

4. *Specify how you will execute to achieve your goals.* Clarify your message, your approach, and your process to contact all of your potential customers. This is the step in which you determine your personal sales strategy for achieving growth goals based on market opportunities.

Shorten Time Spent on Non-sales Calls

How easy is it to waste time on a phone call? Resist the urge to keep talking to anyone who is not a customer, a lead, or involved in sales support. Set time limits, so calls average less than five minutes. Then, limit the number of non-sales calls to a maximum of eighteen a day. Why eighteen? It's a good limit—eighteen five-minute calls take up an hour and a half of your day. Ninety minutes is a reasonable amount of time to spend on non-sales calls. However, if you spend another four minutes on each call, as lower-performing reps tend to do, and increase your number of calls to twenty-five, you lose almost four hours to non-sales calls. This is half of your day, assuming you work eight hours—nearly twenty hours per week, or two weeks every month. When you think about the other calls you're likely to make in the course of a day (your spouse, children, friends, coworkers, and other calls made for personal business), you can see how quickly you can run out of time.

If you have to make internal, non-sales calls, call at times when you know your party will be available and not distracted, so you can resolve your issue quickly. Predetermine the items you need to cover, and check them off during the call. This simple cheat sheet will outline all essential points, keep you focused, and dissuade the other party from engaging in a lot of "yada, yada, yada."

If a call doesn't require personal interaction, call when you know the person is unavailable so that you can make your point in voice mail and not waste time with unnecessary details. You can use this simple trick to save phone time: Call the cell phone number when you want to reach someone. Call the office number when you want to leave a message.

To prove how much time you can save, count the number of non-sales calls you make in a day. Time those calls. Deter-

 Tackle Box

TIPS TO SPEED UP A PHONE CALL

- Have a list of things you want to cover.

- State early that you only have five minutes. If you call, act surprised that you caught them, and say you were only going to leave a message. If they call you, let them know you are in the middle of something and can spare only a few minutes.

- Call right before lunch or right before 5:00 P.M.

- When you call someone, give them the basic facts and then tell them you'll send a follow-up e-mail with the details.

- Always control the flow of the discussion. Do not let the call move onto another topic. If it starts to, ask to schedule another call.

- Set a specific time during the day to make your non-sales calls. You will find you are less verbose and more disciplined if you have many calls to make.

mine how much of the time was actually time well spent. Then develop methods for cutting your unproductive phone time.

 Catch of the Day

Apply shortcuts to non-sales calls only. Be sure to never rush a sales opportunity.

Make Better Use of E-Mail

As a rule, good salespeople are highly verbal. This trait makes you effective, but it can also cause you to waste time. Avoid the opportunity. When making non-sales calls, or trying to explain or resolve issues, simply send an e-mail rather than risk a long conversation. E-mails also give you a paper trail and allow you to make your point without distractions. In many cases, it's the best way to get people to respond quickly.

Don't Waste Time in the Office

If you're a direct sales rep who travels to customer sites, time in the office can be distracting. When in the office, don't get caught up in meaningless chitchat. Avoid being rude or unsocial, but limit idle conversations as much as possible. Set a goal to spend as much time as possible with your customers and prospects, not with your coworkers. Here are some tips to make you more efficient during your time in the office:

1. When unplanned visitors enter your office or workspace, get out of your chair, meet them at the entrance, and continue to stand. You are being polite, yet preventing them from sitting down and getting comfortable in your space. They will get the message and be quick with their conversation.

2. For unwelcome visitors: Plan A—say you have a conference call shortly and need to call for a conference bridge or call-in number. Plan B—move papers around and look busy. People will feel uncomfortable and know that they are interrupting something.

3. Avoid walking around the office to stretch and see who is in—it's a good way to sabotage effective time management.

4. If you have a door, close it. People will typically think twice before interrupting.

5. If you have an administrative assistant (AA), have him or her screen your calls or visitors. You might even forward your calls to your AA.

6. Don't answer every call. If you don't have caller ID, let voice mail pick up. Consider giving your cell phone number only to customers. Give everyone else your work number. You can then answer your cell, because you know it's important, and let the voice mail pick up your internal phone.

7. Get a big cup. If you drink coffee, tea, or water, get an oversized cup so you don't have to make multiple trips to the break room. It's not the walk that's so bad; it's the distractions that may arise on the way there and back.

Use Travel Time Wisely

The airplane, train, or car can be the best place to gain time. Depending on the nature of your sales role, travel time can take up a big percentage of your week. The productivity study cited earlier in the chapter revealed that top reps spend about 15 percent of their time traveling. That equates to a little more than an hour a day, or six hours a week. Add that up over the course of the year, and you get about 300 hours in all. Travel time actually can be substantially higher for reps who travel out of region or state (600 or more hours per year).

Imagine the productivity if you put down the newspaper or non-business book or stopped people-watching in the airport, and used some of this time to do paperwork or expense reporting; return phone calls; or even prospect via a wireless remote connection. You would gain valuable hours and have little interruption. If you travel by car, you can't attempt all of these activities while driving, but you can return calls or listen to training tapes or CDs.

Leverage the People Around You

Many tasks (for example, expense reports, prospecting, meeting follow-up, company and/or industry research) can be delegated to an AA, sales assistant, more junior sales reps, or other support roles. Delegation was difficult for me to learn personally, but it now helps me get many more things accomplished over the course of the day. You may be surprised that others can be as effective as you are—or even more so. You just have to relinquish some control, invest some time in training, and trust them to get the job done. In the meantime, you can focus on the selling activities that only you can do.

CAPTAIN'S LOG

Heed the advice of Tarpon Willie: "You can't learn to fish if you don't have a teacher." Think of delegation as an opportunity to help an AA or junior rep learn, grow, develop critical skills, and prepare for his or her next role.

What Can You Delegate?

The surest way to keep office busywork from eating up your time is this: Have someone else do it! Here are some things you may be able to delegate to others:

Expense reporting and submission. This can eat up a lot of time, and while important to you, it does nothing to drive sales.

Maintaining your calendar. Let your Administrative Assistant (AA) control your calendar. Maintaining a proper calendar helps keep you organized and focused on important tasks, functions, and appointments. You can block off certain hours to attend to critical activities and reserve other hours for meetings and appointments. Your AA will be better at keeping time sacred than you will, and he or she can help screen unwanted activities or "time-stealing predators."

Confirming appointments. Confirm face-to-face appointments a day or two prior to your meeting. You may prefer to call some clients yourself, but let your AA handle the others.

Making copies, proofing, editing, gathering material, and so on. These small administrative tasks can really eat up time. Don't do them—find someone else who will.

Deal crediting. Average performers can waste more than 10 percent of their time ensuring that their deal was properly entered and credited into the system for commission payment. Have your AA create a simple sheet that shows your personal deals and the amount of credit or commission you're received. Are you concerned that your AA will know how much you make? Chances are, he or she knows already. Your job is to show that you're worth the big bucks by working smart and sticking to a disciplined schedule.

Become a Mentor

Can junior sellers help you? Yes! If your organization is set up in this manner, become a mentor to junior sellers. Teach them the ropes, and also use the relationship to gain leverage. The best way to teach someone is to let him or her take on some of the job, such as:

- *Prospecting new customers.* Let junior sellers help you create awareness vehicles. They may have a different approach to give you insight on ways to reach new accounts, younger customers, different types of customers, and so on.
- *Creating new contact lists.*

- *Collecting business cards of potential clients.*
- *Assisting with research and meeting preparation.* Give them tasks that will be a learning experience, but also help you. Examples include researching competitors, building organizational charts of prospect companies, taking notes at meetings you cannot or do not want to attend, and proofing technical materials.

 ## Catch of the Day

Share the recognition you might get as a top seller with the folks who help you. Also, if a meeting goes well and others helped prepare the materials, give them feedback and acknowledge their contribution. Others will be more inclined to continue to help if they feel they are a part of your success. Everyone likes to be associated with a winner.

Treat Your Home Office as a Professional Place

When working at home, act as if you are in the office. Some ways to make sure you do this:

Have your own space. It will help you keep your work functions separate from your personal functions. Make sure you have a separate phone line, fax machine, high-speed line, computer, and printer.

Avoid home chores. Practice discipline! Do not allow yourself to mow the lawn or fix the gate when you have an extra hour between calls.

Wake up to an alarm. Maintain the schedule that you would if you were working in a regular office. Set a time to start work, a time to finish, and a time for lunch and breaks. Do not deviate from the schedule. Don't tell yourself, "Today I'll start at

10:00 A.M. so I can run an errand, and then I'll work till 7:00 P.M. to make it up." You never really make up the lost time, and the errands start to multiply as your self-discipline erodes.

Shower and dress in the morning. Do not work in pajamas. You will be tempted to get involved in non-sales or non-work activities—or worse, go take a nap.

 **Catch of the Day**

Wear your business clothes to your home office. This will help you fight the urge to do household chores; you will not want to get your work clothes dirty.

Establish clear rules with spouse, children, and friends. Often, when working from home, others will desire your time. Let them know you are working and are busy. Use the same techniques mentioned earlier for office time management. I've been asked many times to watch a sleeping baby while my wife runs an errand "real quick." Somehow my sons seem to know when I have an important call and they wake up unexpectedly. At that point, you're stuck!

Organize Your Files, Desk, and Computer

It's easy to neglect putting things in the proper place or attending to important messages or matters in the moment. When papers go unfiled and messages sit in e-mail unanswered, you can quickly feel overwhelmed. You can do two things to avoid this feeling: (1) do not procrastinate on important things; and (2) organize your tasks into groups or buckets.

If you have tasks organized with the most important items first, and tackle them regularly, you are more likely to feel comfortable with your progress and status. My first sales manager used to say, "Keep a list; number your list; complete the first three each day, and lock up the rest in your drawer at night. You will feel good about what you've accomplished, and you'll know the tasks can't follow you home at night."

Properly Plan and Schedule to Maximize Contacts with Prospects

Tarpon Willie says, "The more time you can create for yourself, the more fish you can catch." This may sound like a simple statement, but it is profound. While you can't create time, you can remove items that are causing you to waste time, or organize your time to take advantage of when the "fish are biting." The best anglers know when to fish (fast-moving tides) and when to scout or move to the next spot (slow-moving tides).

Sales reps must adhere to the same principles. Top salespeople schedule their work week according to their buyers' week to maximize the best use of their time. Effectively managing your time in sales is not only about curtailing non-sales activities. Poorly timing your business development activities can be another time waster. You must figure out all the "whens," including when to canvas a territory, when to pick up the phone, when to make sales presentations, and when to deliver the goods to the buyers.

Here's how to maximize the likelihood that there will be someone there to take your call:

1. Call early in the morning, before your customer's day starts and meetings and other events devour the time.
2. If your customers travel, they may avoid the Monday morning and Friday afternoon crunch. Try reaching them then.

3. Try lunch time. These days, many people eat at their desk.

4. Call after 5:00 P.M. Not many meetings are scheduled after 5:00 P.M., and in many cases, your customers are finishing up their day and may have a few minutes.

THIS AIN'T NO FISH TALE!

I learned an important lesson in my first job as a business development rep. Bill, a family friend, headed up purchasing for a telecom company. He was aware of my new role and expressed interest in my company's products and services. He asked me to give him a call as soon as I got acclimated. When I finished my training, Bill was one of the first calls I made. When I reached his voice mail, I left a message, figuring he would call me right back. Two days passed with no response. On the third day, I called again and left another message. When all my calls went unreturned, I concluded that Bill hadn't gotten my messages. So the next week I called on Monday, Tuesday, and Wednesday. Three weeks went by with still no response from Bill. After numerous messages and a couple of e-mails, I felt slighted and figured Bill really wasn't interested. So I moved on to other accounts. As I was leaving the office on a Friday afternoon, I picked up the phone to give Bill one more try. He answered the phone and lit up when he heard my name. He apologized for not returning my calls, explaining that it was his busy season. At that point, we had a great conversation and, in time, I made a nice sale.

This experience taught me that some days are better than others when calling clients. A productive conversation requires a focused listener who is in the office and open to hearing what you have to say.

Catch of the Day

Anecdotal evidence shows that prospective customers are more likely to make a purchase or take a sales call on Thursdays and Fridays. Earlier in the week, they are more likely to be traveling. On Friday, you have a much higher percentage of finding buyers in the office, cleaning up matters from the week. So go where the fish are and make contact when they are there.

Are You a Time Waster or Time Investor?

Try the following quiz to find out whether you are wasting time or investing your time during your work week. For each statement, note whether it is something you often do ("O"), sometimes do ("S"), or never do ("N").

1. I like to socialize with my friends in the office. _____
2. I give my friends my e-mail address. _____
3. I send non-work-related e-mails from my work e-mail address. _____
4. I read the news and check stock quotes while at work. _____
5. I go out of the office every day for lunch. _____
6. I take lunch breaks that last more than one hour. _____
7. I start getting ready to leave work before 5:00 P.M. _____
8. It takes me a while to get started once I am at the office. _____
9. I take many breaks during the day. _____
10. I spend a lot of time on the phone that is not business related. _____

11. I often schedule personal appointments or doctor appointments to fall during business hours. ____
12. I attend many non-sales-related meetings during the day. ____
13. I go to many training classes during the day. ____
14. After a sales call, I head home rather than go back to the office. ____
15. I try to combine a bit of sightseeing with all of my sales calls. ____
16. I speak to my spouse more than twice a day while at work. ____
17. I cut out early on Friday afternoons to play golf, run errands, or pick up the kids. ____
18. I spend time at work thinking about all the personal things going on in my life. ____
19. I spend time thinking about corporate politics or my standing in the company. ____
20. I volunteer for non-sales-related functions that cut into my business development time. ____

How do you measure up? For every "N/never," give yourself two points; for every "S/sometimes," give yourself one point; for every "O/often," give yourself zero points.

- **40–31 POINTS:** Your ability to focus on selling activities and to block out items that can distract you from your mission is excellent. Keep the discipline, and continue to lead by example. More than likely, you consistently have strong results.
- **30–21 POINTS:** Your time management skills are good. However, you could be much more successful if you stopped doing the things that are draining your sales time and your earning power. Pick three items and,

over the next week, commit to resisting them. Once you build your discipline in these areas, choose three more and work on those.

- **20 POINTS OR LESS:** You must be unhappy in your job. Something either in your makeup or in the job is causing you to focus on the wrong things and is making you ineffective. You need to determine whether you want to stay in sales or start a new career. If you decide to stay put, then you need to rededicate yourself to selling.

CHAPTER FIVE

Chum the Water

CREATE AWARENESS FOR YOUR PRODUCT OR OFFERING

Tarpon Willie and I were drifting along the shore in his boat. The water was still and as smooth as glass, reflecting a brilliant blue sky. The only sound was a gull in the distance. Our poles were up, with their lines disappearing into the ocean. There wasn't a ripple or wave in sight. Willie turned to me and said, "This is a beautiful postcard picture, but we're here to fish, not admire the scenery! We've been out on the water for two hours without a bite. If we want to catch fish, we have two options: We can start chumming the water or we can motor to another location. We're already here, so why not throw out some chum and see what happens?" Since I know always to follow Willie's advice, I cut up some chum and tossed it in the water. Within fifteen minutes, we had a bite, and the fish kept finding us all day.

> **CAPTAIN'S LOG**
> "It's better to pull the anchor fifteen times in a day than sit and let the fish come to you—because they won't. And trust me, I know that anchor is heavy!"— Tarpon Willie

Fishermen use chum, or fish parts, to lure fish to their boat and increase their chances of catching their limit. Cutting up dead fish isn't a fun or desirable task, but it gets results:

chum dramatically increases the probability of catching fish by enticing them to swim closer to check out the activity.

In sales, chum is the SOV (something of value) that attracts customers to the product or offering. The key is to give customers just enough information and guidance to pique their interest and stimulate demand, but not totally fulfill their needs. Customers won't buy a bigger product if they fill up on giveaways. Instead, an SOV should engage and persuade customers to "window-shop" while you strive to understand their needs and issues through careful questions and casual, but focused, conversation.

Identify and Create the Most Effective SOV

In the best case, the SOV will spur a customer to seek you out for more information; in the worse case, SOV reminds a customer that you're around. SOV stimulates a customer's interest in the same way that chum arouses fish. When times are slow, creating SOV is especially effective to make you feel that you're "doing something" to generate interest down the line.

SOV can consist of many different things, from free samples to product testimonials. You can increase your chances of attracting customers by creating your own SOV to lure prospects to your boat. It's easier than it sounds, and it's an area in which salespeople can excel.

These days, it's a rare deal that isn't highly competitive. When considering a purchase, most companies seek three to five bids or shop around until they hear something they like. So whether you're responding to a formal RFP (request for proposal) or discussing your product or offer at a meeting, be ready to stand out. Make sure your SOV is designed to grab your prospect's interest, and not sink to the "circular file."

Tackle Box

CHUM SELECTION TIPS

The type of SOV you use depends on your product; your company or organization; your audience; and your budget. Be prepared to chum each time you go "fishing" for customers by knowing the answers to the following questions:

- **Your product.** Is your product transactional, or does it have a long sales cycle? How much will the customer buy?
- **Your company or organization.** What are your company's marketing policies? What parameters do you need to follow? Do you have the authority to create your own chum?
- **Your audience.** Who are you trying to reach?
- **Your budget.** How much money and time is available to create and deliver the chum?

Use the SOVs Top Sellers Prefer

Tarpon Willie says, "Junk attracts junk; make sure your chum is truly of value." The following seven simple SOVs are great examples of chum that can get you a bite—or more:

- Free or sample products
- Informational material about you, your company, your product, customer testimonials, and your successes
- Competitor and industry information
- Self-assessment tools, such as audits
- Content surveys and best practices
- Workshops
- Conferences

THIS AIN'T NO FISH TALE!

Several years ago, I had the chance to observe two highly successful software sales reps present their SOV to prospects on two separate sales calls. Both situations were tough sells—extremely competitive sales to sophisticated, discriminating buyers. Both reps subsequently closed their deals. What separated them from the pack was simple: they differentiated themselves and were well prepared—from their professional attire to their well-thought-out presentations. In one case, "Andy" closed his deal through a simple product demo customized with client pricing and the client's logo. On a different sales call, "Jenn" came armed with customer survey results that showcased productivity gains among companies that used her product. She supplemented the results with industry facts, customer references, and compelling data that built a strong case for ROI (return on investment). Jenn also had a satisfied customer standing by to take a phone call if her prospect wanted a live testimonial.

Both presentations demonstrated awareness of the customers' issues and needs. The reps' preparation conveyed compelling attention to the details. Following the second presentation, I quizzed the customer about their reaction. The customer responded, "This presentation was hard to beat. She knows my industry, was professional, and came armed with the facts . . . and we love facts." And it's true—people love facts and information, so always be prepared and have the data at hand.

In the following sections, we'll consider the best ways to make use of each of these SOVs.

SOV #1: Free or Sample Products

Complimentary product samples or services are a great way to showcase your product capabilities and/or your abilities. Think in terms of the chum: giving the fish a nibble makes them want more. It's the same with samples; if customers are unsure of your product's capabilities, give them a sample so they see how it works or performs. If you're selling professional services, your SOV may be some free advice. Offering your customer a taste of what they will receive is very valuable, especially if your product or offer is as good as you think.

When offering something "free":

- *Never give away so much that you risk filling up your customer.* Give your customers just enough to see your product in action or to get a taste of your approach. Make sure they understand that this is just a sample, allowing them to discover that your product meets their needs or works in a way that provides value. Let them see that your objective is their comfort and satisfaction with your product or service.
- *Provide a small quantity or offer a limited trial period.* For example, "Try it risk free for thirty days." The limited trial encourages them to pay if they choose to keep the product.
- *Don't confuse a free sample with discounting and/or a "freebie" in order to close a sale.* Avoid discounting and throwing in freebies unless they are figured into your margin and cost. Initial discounts encourage your buyers to keep

asking for them with each renewal or follow-on sale. Sell the customers on the value of your product. If they start hinting for freebies and discounts, go back to the value proposition—the tangible results a customer gets from using your product or service—and restate the benefits that your product offers. Remember, you got to this point based upon value; don't be pulled back to level one. In addition, focusing on value will dampen the emotional aspect of the negotiations. See the Tackle Box below for

 Tackle Box

HOW TO RESPOND WHEN A CUSTOMER WANTS MORE FREEBIES OR A DEEPER DISCOUNT

Response #1: Stress the Quality. "I realize that you're concerned about price. That's one reason we've priced at this level. I want to understand your concerns and ensure that you fully understand all that you are getting for this price. Let me reiterate that our product is better suited for your needs based upon XYZ. We also adhere to a better quality standard; we use the most up-to-date technologies [or whatever applies]. All of these considerations need to be factored into the price."

Response #2: Re-explain and Reinforce the Discount. "I fully understand your pricing concerns and I've taken them into account. Given the term of the contract, the quantity of your purchase, and the fact that you're a great customer, I've provided a discount. Perhaps I didn't fully describe what you are getting for this discounted price, so let me describe it again. Once you see how we did the pricing, I think you'll agree that you're getting a great deal."

ways to respond when the customer continues to request a discount or freebie.

As a kid, I remember throwing bread in the water near the dock of a lake to catch brim (aka bluegill, bream, or coppernose). The brim would school and devour the bread. But as soon as I lowered my hook in the water, worm and all, the brim turned up their collective noses and swam away. Had they filled up on bread? Maybe—or was it the change in bait, from bread to a worm? I was never quite sure, but I never made the mistake again. I learned to limit my chumming rather than let the fish (or customer) fill up on freebies.

SOV #2: Informational Material About You, Your Company, Your Product

Positive or influential information geared to better position you, your company, and your product or offer is probably one of the easiest forms of SOVs to create. It is also one of the easiest to botch. Make certain that you have the following information at hand.

Information About You

Always have your bio handy. A bio is not a resume; it presents personal and professional information about you and your experiences that will help a customer differentiate you from others. A bio can take a more creative approach and format than a resume, and it can be more personal. Customize your bio to highlight your experience as it relates to your audience. Include your bio in all information packets that go to prospects. In many instances, when all else is equal, a bio can be the deciding factor that differentiates you from the competition. Tarpon Willie always says, "People like to fish with people they know and like." So it is with doing business—think of your bio as the first step in getting prospects to know you, like you, and trust you.

Include the following in your bio:

1. History of your work experience—It's not necessary to list all employers; highlight the experience that will show your customers that you know their business
2. Professional and personal highlights
3. Major accomplishments in your field
4. Any relevant facts that might interest and create a bond between you and your prospects

Information About Your Company

Seems like a no-brainer, but I'm continually amazed at how many companies and salespeople do not have the right information about their company on hand. Most companies have a marketing department that creates this material and distributes it to the sales force. If this is the case, great! However, in some cases, sales reps are tasked with creating their own. In either case, customize the material to focus on the areas important to your customer. Customization is not about creating glossy materials, but rather focusing on facts salient to your prospects, such as "We've been in business for thirty-five years," "We are the largest manufacturer of cardboard boxes in the world," or "We serve three of the five largest U.S. airlines." Customize to show you are a reputable, secure business, poised to meet the customers' specific needs.

Information About Your Product

At the end of the day, it's all about the product. Whether the product is a widget or your professional services, let it showcase itself through a product demonstration and/or product materials. In a product demonstration, keep in mind that you are *not* the main attraction. When you promise a demo, make sure you deliver a demo—not a presentation delivered by you about the product. Your role is facilitator. The customers are buying the physical object, so position the demo according to their needs, and let the product match up with the buyers and their expectations.

With product information materials, some of the same principles apply: Always emphasize what is important to your customer, and make sure the pitch is as customized as possible. Be certain that your materials truly demonstrate your product's capabilities, especially if you're not doing a demo. Include success stories, customer testimonials, and those "it" factors that differentiate your product. If you're handed marketing material that doesn't include these points, create your own "verbal materials" to get the story told.

Simple things such as, "This is where you would get the most value," "This is how your competitors use the product," or even explaining how anyone can use the product will go a long way toward personalizing your merchandise.

CAPTAIN'S LOG

Tarpon Willie says: "Fish don't talk, but if you listen closely, they will tell you when they're hungry." Same with customers: when people are considering a purchase, they don't always say so directly; they want you to figure it out. Keep in mind the factors that typically differentiate a company: product, price, quality, stability, ease of doing business, company personnel, and value. How do you find out what is most important to your prospect? Do your research prior to marketing to the customer. You can also listen carefully—or ask them!

When it comes to product information:

- Keep a file of materials that have worked best for you, with notes about the ways that you have customized them.
- Even if you do not create the marketing materials, you can influence them if you provide good feedback about what works and what doesn't.
- Always supplement your demos and information with your stories—your "verbal material."

Ask your customers what they thought of your material and your demo. This feedback can help you tailor your approach for your next prospect.

Customer Testimonials

Are your customers happy with you? If they are, use that goodwill to your advantage. Chapter 3 outlined the advantages of making customers part of your team. If they can't attend a sales meeting in person, their presence can still be felt through testimonials in your chum. Ask them to share

THIS AIN'T NO FISH TALE!

On a ride-along, I observed a rep who pulled out her laptop on a sales call and dazzled her prospect with a flashy PowerPoint demonstration about how her product was tailor-made to create customer success. The presentation concluded with the client's logo superimposed on shots from a trade magazine bearing the caption: "'Joe Client' Named Executive of the Year for Increasing His Company's Shareholder Wealth Three-fold." The rep won the deal, beating out much larger competitors.

their experience about how well you, your company, or your product meets their needs. For greatest impact, try to match up customers in similar businesses or those with similar needs and issues. At a minimum, always touch on customer examples—provide detail about the way a customer uses your product, including customer quotes. A better way is to invite a prospect to call a customer and get the story straight from that person. Direct conversation enables the prospect to ask questions without reservation.

 ## Catch of the Day

Do not pay or offer discounts to customers for their testimonial. Use customers who want to help because they believe in your offering. If you cloud testimonials with incentives, you run the risk of getting customers who have ulterior motives.

Believe it or not, a saltwater fish called a cobia (aka lemon fish) gives its own "client testimonials"—and the other fish listen. When hooked, this species of fish sends out signals that attract more cobia. When cobia hear a fellow fish's calls, they'll swim to the site of the commotion, and, attracted by the excitement, are likely to bite.

When it comes to customer testimonials:

- Promote reputable customers with recognizable names and good track records.
- Match customers who share similar issues, desire the same features, or are in similar industries.
- Make sure your customers are "testifying" because they are sold on the product's value, not just doing you a favor.
- Match customers in the same pricing category—they will talk price whether you ask them to or not.

SOV #3: Competitor and Industry Information (Trends and Issues)

Differentiate yourself by being conversant about your prospect's competitors. Providing facts about their industry and other trends and issues related to your prospects makes you a figure of trust and authority—enabling you to position your product or service with greater influence. Such information is available through many sources, including Web sites, ana-

 Tackle Box

PRODUCT DEMONSTRATION BEST PRACTICES

Always customize or plan your demo to match the specific needs of the client. Whether in the setup or through the configuration of your demonstration, take the extra time to show how your product or service would specifically serve the customer's situation. Show that you are truly interested in the client's business and that you care about customer satisfaction. Customization does *not* mean omitting portions of the sales pitch that do not apply; it means creating a demo specific to the customer, without extraneous information.

Always be well prepared, well rehearsed, and somewhat scripted in your approach. (But don't sound scripted.) Solid prep work will allow you to answer questions, remain focused, and meet your objectives. Product demos can get off-message quickly if a prospect poses difficult questions that you can't answer, or wants to "off-road" by pushing different buttons or requesting a different demo than you'd planned. To avoid this, prior to the demo clarify which specific features the company would like to see, questions

lysts' reports, company annual reports, surveys, customers, friends, and other salespeople.

Being knowledgeable does *not* mean sharing confidential information or breaking customer confidence; it means understanding where the market or industry is heading and how your prospect's chief rivals are meeting these market demands. Do not share secrets; share only publicly available data, or data gathered from customers that those customers might not mind being made public, or would share themselves.

 Tackle Box *(continued)*

it may have, and its expectations about the demo. These queries help you set the stage before the curtain goes up. If you do get questions or requests that are outside of your planned presentation, redirect the focus.

For example, you might say, "Oh, that is a great request. Unfortunately, when we set up this customized demo, we focused exclusively on this view. We are happy to go in that direction if you would like; we will just have to reconfigure our presentation." Of course, if you can do so right then and you have the capabilities, you should.

Involve the prospect as much as possible. Let your customer "drive." No one method is more effective at improving your chances of winning the business than is letting your customer try out your product. You can highlight how easy it is to use, how good it feels or how well it responds, and how well you think it will meet the company's needs. If you're confident that the product matches those needs, let the prospect try it out solo, without looking over his or her shoulder.

Most companies are very interested in keeping pace with their competitors and peers. They are curious about others' new offerings, products, or pricing, as well as industry trends. If you can provide this information, you provide a great service, and it shows you are well prepared and want their business. You'll also find that your prospects are not shy about calling themselves a "me-too industry" or "a tag-along type." They want to know what others are doing and what the latest trends might be. For example, depending on your product and your prospect's industry, information such as the following can arouse a prospect's interest:

CAPTAIN'S LOG

Tarpon Willie says, "Whatever move you make on the water, make sure it is done with the fish in mind." The same holds true for sales—whatever informational point you use, make sure it relates back to your product.

- Why large wireless companies are buying more computer servers.
- Why the pharmaceutical industry is facing a hiring challenge.
- What auto dealers are doing to sell more cars.
- How software is increasing employee productivity and accelerating sales.
- What the key trends and issues are in the printing business.

SOV #4: Self-Assessment Tools

Self-assessment tools are a good way to get participation and feedback from a prospect without making them feel threatened or like they are being "sold to." Self-assessments allow you to get critical information about areas of concern, which may help you position your product or service against your prospects' issues.

The typical self-assessment tool is a simple questionnaire enabling a company to rate itself against best practices, industry norms, or even its own mission statement or corporate objectives. More advanced self-assessment tools provide a grading scale that a prospect can use to determine an overall score and rate itself against others.

When using self-assessment tools:

- Don't make them too long or too complicated; your prospects may not finish the test.
- Always structure the quiz in a way that is not critical or judgmental; your quiz takers are usually hard enough on themselves.
- Build in questions that allow quiz takers to see some of their good qualities. They have done many things right, so make sure you point that out.
- Give them some simple advice or simple suggestions on how to get better.
- Always include your contact information in any self-assessment tool.

For an example of a self-assessment tool, see the Chummer Quiz at the end of Chapter 6.

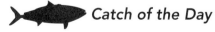 **Catch of the Day**

Since no one is perfect, some deficiency may be exposed during the assessment. Use that revelation not to focus on the deficiencies, but to close the gap with your product or service.

SOV #5: Content Surveys and Best Practices

Content surveys and best practices present some of the best SOV available when trying to engage customers or prospects in conversations. Surveys present nonthreatening, value-add material that will generate interest because of the business or competitive intelligence they can provide. A typical content or best practice survey identifies key areas of interest and establishes a baseline reflecting other companies' or world-class practices. The best surveys are well thought out and include topics or practices that will stimulate discussion.

For customers or other survey participants, a survey provides free-of-charge information that adds value to their business. Participation in the survey requires a limited time commitment in exchange for competitive best practices that are hard to find or don't exist elsewhere. To create greater demand for the survey and the data that it will contain, it's helpful to give participants an opportunity to structure or add important questions or requirements to the survey.

 *Catch of the Day*

A survey gives you a great non-selling reason to meet and/or call a prospect, as well as license to continue the conversation multiple times. Points of contact: (1) invite the prospect to participate; (2) meet or call to conduct the survey; (3) call again to follow up with additional questions; (4) visit, to share results; and (5) make a final contact and get the sale.

As the creator of the survey, you broaden your industry knowledge and arm yourself with key industry facts, making new contacts in the process. Determine survey topics by using the following tips:

- Asking the participants.
- Using topics that are not addressed elsewhere, yet are important.
- Using topics that relate to you, your company, or your product or offer.
- Developing topics that stimulate discussion or may even be divisive to a certain extent.

As an example of a survey, see the "2007 Software Purchasing Trends in the High-Tech Industry" on pages 104–105.

SOV #6: Workshops

Workshops straddle the line by being both an offering and a means for delivering an SOV to existing and potential customers. A workshop can be tailored and offered to a single company, or designed for multiple companies.

Single company: A workshop targeted to a specific company invites a group of decision-makers from one company to sit in an open forum and discuss their issues, enabling you to facilitate the conversation. You may host the workshop free of charge to promote your products or service, or you may charge participants to attend. Typically, in a free workshop, you should focus on the key issues or problems a company faces, and offer help. When facilitating the workshop, always position your product or offering to match the key issues or trends that the workshop addresses. If you are spending your time and effort to facilitate the workshop, make sure you position yourself to address the prospect's need.

When hosting a paid workshop, most of the above holds true except that you may do less positioning and instead take the role of expert or knowledgeable industry source. The

2007 SOFTWARE PURCHASING TRENDS IN THE HIGH-TECH INDUSTRY

XYZ Company would like to invite you to participate in a complimentary High-Tech Software Best Practices Benchmarking Survey. The survey is being conducted over the next four weeks to identify some of the key trends in software purchasing in the high-tech industry.

Survey Objectives and Scope: The survey will focus on key software purchasing practices in the high-tech market and includes some of the following items:

- How much do high-tech companies allocate for software purchases on a yearly basis?

- How do they pay for the software? (i.e., capital expense versus monthly expense)

- Who manages the purchasing process? (i.e., IT, Finance, Business Unit or Procurement)

Participant Benefits: Participation is free of charge and you will receive a detailed report that will include both quantitative and qualitative productivity benchmark information. Included in this report will be observations about how your company compares to other companies and to the key issues or trends common in the market today.

All of your individual company data points will remain confidential and will not be shared with any other individual participant. The data that will be included in the report will be identified by generic titles and/or reported at an aggregate level.

Participating Companies: The following companies have either been invited or agreed to participate: Company A, Company B, Company C, Company D, Company E, Company F, Company G.

The Survey Process: The survey will be conducted in two simple phases: The first phase is a short electronic survey instrument that we will send out via e-mail. The second phase will be a 30-minute follow-up interview to help clarify the data provided in the electronic survey instrument and confirm its accuracy.

Thanks again for your consideration. Our participants are excited about conducting a great survey this year. To register or get more information, please contact me at xxx-xxx-xxxx or at *Jdimisa@sibson.com.*

I look forward to hearing back from you and answering any questions you may have.

Best Regards,

Joe DiMisa
Sibson Consulting

participants are paying you to facilitate and offer expert opinion, not position your product or offer. If they trust you and buy into your effectiveness and expertise, they most likely will buy into your product or offer, too.

Multiple companies: In a multiple-company workshop, a group of similar companies with similar issues come together to compare notes and learn from one another's experiences. As with the single-company workshop, the trick is to position yourself as the facilitator. Multiple-company participation creates networking opportunities for your clients and allows them to discuss their issues with other companies who have the same problems. The real value with this form of SOV is that you assemble a great group of people to discuss their issues. Content is important, but the best value is the participants' ability to hear other companies' experiences and compare these facts with their own situations.

Keep these points in mind for effective workshops:

- Make the workshop exclusive.
- Invite similar levels (peers should be of equal status).
- Limit attendance to twenty-five people.
- Let the participants do the talking.
- Don't let one participant do all the talking.

SOV #7: Conferences

Conferences are another great SOV that also qualify as a delivery mechanism. Conferences are usually focused by industry, product, or topic and attract many similar types of influencers or buyers. The key with conferences is choosing the right one to attend or to sponsor. When you speak or exhibit at a conference, you have a captive audience of targeted, potential customers. Take advantage of this heightened exposure by offering enticing information that is attractive to attendees at all levels of an organization.

 ## Catch of the Day

Offering a free consultation or self-audit assessment is a great way of encouraging prospects to call you to discuss their needs or the results of their self-audit.

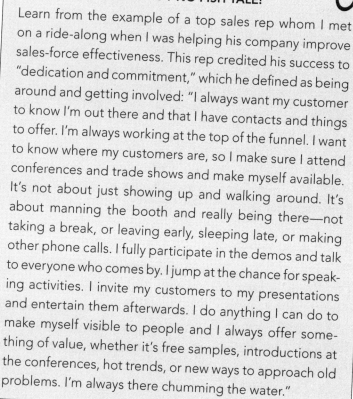

THIS AIN'T NO FISH TALE!

Learn from the example of a top sales rep whom I met on a ride-along when I was helping his company improve sales-force effectiveness. This rep credited his success to "dedication and commitment," which he defined as being around and getting involved: "I always want my customer to know I'm out there and that I have contacts and things to offer. I'm always working at the top of the funnel. I want to know where my customers are, so I make sure I attend conferences and trade shows and make myself available. It's not about just showing up and walking around. It's about manning the booth and really being there—not taking a break, or leaving early, sleeping late, or making other phone calls. I fully participate in the demos and talk to everyone who comes by. I jump at the chance for speaking activities. I invite my customers to my presentations and entertain them afterwards. I do anything I can do to make myself visible to people and I always offer something of value, whether it's free samples, introductions at the conferences, hot trends, or new ways to approach old problems. I'm always there chumming the water."

A junior executive who has little decision-making authority may attend your seminar or pick up your brochure and business card and pass it along to a higher-level executive who has buying approval.

 ## Catch of the Day

A sales rep's "funnel," aka "pipeline," describes the total amount of potential revenue from identified and/or qualified sales opportunities. "Funnel" is used more often than "pipeline," but "pipeline" refers to the total amount of potential, whereas "funnel" has stages of qualifications. "Top of the funnel" means all the activities a rep does to generate excitement. Depending on the business, this could include cold calling, industry networking, writing articles, giving speeches, sending out mailings, and entertaining potential customers. When these activities create awareness and the rep is able to qualify opportunities, those opportunities are counted in the funnel. Sales are the output of the funnel.

Get Your Name Out There

If you're attending a conference but not exhibiting or sponsoring it, the following tricks will help you to meet potential and current clients.

1. *Always wear your company logo shirt, hat, or jacket.* This distinctive apparel gets you noticed and creates a presence for you and your company. I am always surprised at how many questions a shirt or jacket can generate. Also, ask about others' logo attire. A simple comment can start a conversation and enable you to talk about your company when the conversation switches to your logo.

2. *In advance of your conference trip, make lunch or dinner plans with a select group of conference participants.* Include cur-

THIS AIN'T NO FISH TALE!

What's the value of chum? I was once looking for a contractor to build a deck on my home. I interviewed contractors referred by neighbors, those with eye-catching ads, and anyone who would show up and give me a bid, and I narrowed the pool to three. Their bids were similar and their references checked out, but I was stuck. While I was mulling my options, one of the contractors called and asked if I had made a decision. I replied that I was in the process and would get back to him soon. He queried me further, asking whether I was considering price, quality, timing, or other factors. I admitted that I had three good candidates and wanted to sleep on it. "I can appreciate that," he replied. Then he asked me if I'd taken a ride around the neighborhood. "I have a few projects in your area right now. Many are repeat customers. One was a project similar to yours. I know that client would be happy to answer questions you might have about my work." Later that day, in my mailbox, I found a packet of letters from the Better Business Bureau, contract supply companies, and neighborhood associations that attested to the contractor's quality. The envelope bore a personal note: "Joe, if you haven't made a decision by this weekend, please come by the Georgia Home Show and visit my booth. We have a display of our work, plus articles from local newspapers. We've been recognized as one of the largest and fastest-growing contractors in the state."

I was impressed—not only with the material and his experience, but also with his professionalism. I figured if he was as good at building as he was at selling, I had found a winner. The deck turned out great. He clearly had the right stuff—from the chum to the service—and knew how to hit all of my needs as a customer.

rent clients or prospects, or a combination of the two. Select a restaurant with a good reputation that's appropriate for business. Most conference attendees welcome a chance for a nice dinner when someone else picks up the check.

3. *Attend all of the social functions, breakouts, or group gatherings you can.* Many buyers attend these functions to get to know potential suppliers, and build relationships with them. Take advantage of all opportunities to meet and greet these people. Also, buyers may be on overload from the pitch of conference sponsors and welcome the insight of participants who did not sponsor the event.

CHAPTER SIX

Put Your Lines in the Water

*QUALIFY YOUR LEADS AND POSITION YOURSELF
TO MEET THEIR NEEDS*

Flying home from a business trip at the end of a hectic week, I checked my cell phone voice mail just as the 747 rolled into the arrival gate. The first message was from Tarpon Willie: "Let's go catch some grouper. See you at six on Saturday."

By 6:30 Saturday morning, Tarpon Willie and I were on the water catching bait. As soon as we had enough bait to entice a hefty catch of grouper, we motored over to our favorite spot. I took advantage of the early morning haze to vent a bit on the frustrations of my work week: a lot of travel, a lot of meeting and greeting, but no firm opportunities or real issues to help solve.

> **CAPTAIN'S LOG**
>
> *"Sure, you can go out and try to catch three different types of fish, but it's a heck of a lot easier to catch three fish of the same type."*
> —Tarpon Willie

Tarpon Willie regarded me shrewdly. "Sounds like you were trying to bring home redfish, flounder, and Spanish mackerel all in one day," he observed. "Clients aren't so different from fish, you know; they have different patterns, different cycles, and spots for congregating. Focus in on one type of catch; you'll bring home one and probably more."

He was about to say more when a tug on his line demanded his attention. Within minutes he reeled in a good-looking grouper. "I'll be darned, the first of the day, and it's a keeper! To finish my observation," he chuckled, "targeting is key!" By day's end, we'd caught our limit of grouper and headed home.

With the wisdom instilled in me by Tarpon Willie, I now selectively target my potential catch on and off the water. I waste less time, sacrifice less chum, and burn a lot less travel time. Truth be told, I catch a lot more too!

Make the Most of Your SOV: Identify the Target Market

In Chapter 5, you learned how to create chum that will stimulate interest from potential buyers. Now let's put that chum to use. People won't buy your product or service if they have no interest in it. The secret is to determine your market and target it with the SOV that's most effective and easily leveraged. This process is known as market segmentation.

Chapter 1 talked about grouping accounts for leverage to get a solid handle on commonalities and customer buying preferences. You can take that a step further and use these groupings or market segments to make decisions about how to align your resources, time, sales pitch, and business process to the buying characteristics of different buyers.

Top sellers know time is precious. They want leads that have a high probability of closing. As Tarpon Willie might say, "They throw their chum in the right spots, so it gets to the right fish; they don't let catfish spoil their day." In contrast, less experienced reps are enamored of the activities at the top of the sales funnel. They often expend significant energy and time generating leads, but have less success closing deals and making quota.

Segment Target Accounts to Focus Your Chum

Market segmentation involves identifying groups of customers with similar needs and buying preferences. Segmentation gives you leverage and allows you to assess and group customers according to certain profiles. These profiles can

---

THIS AIN'T NO FISH TALE!

"Molly" sold a software product to call centers. With about four years of experience, Molly possessed all the traits of a successful rep, yet she was on the short list of those being eyed for a "pink slip." I had been asked to ride along and assess her abilities before the final "go or grow" decision was made. On the job, Molly was excited to talk to anyone who had a call center. She was effective at getting leads, creating awareness, and closing deals. She related well to customers, could diagnose their issues, and communicate how her product would meet their needs. She was a gifted salesperson with a high close rate. So what was the problem? Fact is, she never met her quota. She expended her effort on prospects that were too small. With fewer employees, the companies required fewer license rights. In fact, her customers were so small that Molly would need to sell fifteen accounts per month to make quota. In contrast, the top sellers averaged four sales a month. Molly had the skills, but she needed coaching on how to segment and target her accounts.

provide insights into the customers' needs and preferences for various product and/or service offerings.

Successful segmentation involves the following four steps:

1. Develop a profile of the type of customers you are seeking or are most likely to encounter within your market. Define the profile by determining the following:

- What do the customers do; how are they successful?
- How would the customers view your SOV or your product?
- How will your SOV influence them, or how would your product influence their performance? In other words, what are the key benefits to the customers?
- How would the customers use your SOV or product?
- Who are the decision-makers in the customers' organizations? What are their priorities and preferences?

2. Group customers of similar business profiles into segments, such as by industry, product, product or service application, size, or geography.

3. Match profiles to customers' buying needs and know why they buy. Identify why customers would want your product—for example, features or functions; the package of services; price; or quality. Secondary reasons might include your sales and marketing support, distribution and logistical support, or presale/postsale product support.

4. Apply market segmentation by aligning your energy and time to leverage your SOV. Invest your time in the customers that have the most potential, impact, or similar characteristics.

In many cases, targeting an industry is not enough, because each company within the industry and each business unit within each of those companies has different issues and different goals. Top salespeople discern those different goals and position their product accordingly, chumming the water for their specific catch. The chum presented may focus on cost efficiencies, practicalities, fulfillment and delivery, or P&L (profit and loss). When creating awareness through SOV, successful sellers tailor the material or pitch to match the specific needs and interests of the prospect. Don't get hung up on creating the perfect SOV; you're a salesperson, and you can sell the SOV you have.

Craft your message to the right customers in a way that will encourage them to buy your product or service. Existing clients are more responsive because they already know you. Scrutinize your database of current and past customers, and

CAPTAIN'S LOG
Tarpon Willie says, "Get the chum out of the boat and into the water before it starts to smell." Don't squander your SOV—use it quickly and wisely.

identify their common characteristics. Then use that information as a road map for identifying potential new customers.

If you don't have a database, create one by going through old receipts, your collection of business cards, phone lists, your day planner, and so on, to record existing and potential customers. Make sure all the contact names and addresses are complete and correct. Categorize your target market into potential, current, and past customers.

Get Your SOV to the Right People

In my years of consulting with sales organizations, I've seen lots of great chum, but often it goes to waste due to poor distribution. The SOV may be ready for the taking, but it doesn't get presented correctly—or worst case, doesn't get presented at all. Consultants may be the worst offenders. Consultants create a lot of "thought leadership" content that never gets out of the files or off the hard drive. Consultants have more articles, best practices, benchmark studies, and surveys than can ever be used. The problem is, consultants, by nature, are thinkers. They love to create; they're often reluctant to sell.

To get chum in the water, fishermen use their hand, a chum bucket, or an old-fashioned meat grinder attached to the boat. I've even used a child's plastic baseball bat with a cut-off end. Crusty old salts know to place chum strategically in the water over their fishing spot, or they hang a bag opposite the tide so the chum will flow toward their poles.

Just as there are a variety of ways to put out chum for fish, there are many vehicles for delivering your SOV to your target market, whether it is via direct mail, e-mail, face-to-face meetings, phone calls, workshops, or conferences. Successful sales reps continually evaluate the pros and cons of each method in relation to their particular SOV.

 **Catch of the Day**

Don't become a "consultant." Instead, embrace your sales ability; always remember that first and foremost, you're a salesperson. Take the available SOV and do a bangup job distributing and positioning it.

Direct Mail

Direct mail is a written communication, such as a sales letter, brochure, or postcard that is mailed to a current or prospective customer to elicit a response to buy a product or service. You can use direct mail communications for the following purposes:

- To tell prospective customers about your business
- To tell current customers about a special offer or other promotion
- To remind lapsed customers about your business and include a special offer to renew their interest.

A direct mail list consists of companies or people who have ordered your type of product or service in the past and have a proven history of being responsive. You can buy industry-specific lists through list brokers sorted according to the purchase, price, demographics, and psychographics, so you can target your mailing to an extremely responsive audience.

If your SOV is a sales letter, it must:

- Target the right audience
- Contain the right message
- Be written in the right style

 Tackle Box

CHUM POSITIONING TACTICS

- Send an off-size, one-page letter or postcard stating interesting facts that require prospects to follow up.

- Personalize your letter by using the prospect's name.

- Use lots of white space and break up paragraphs with attention-grabbing subheads.

- Differentiate it—the more provocative and attention-grabbing it is, the more likely it will be noticed and read.

- Include gimmicks, such as a day planner, calendar, coupon, or magnet to get noticed.

If your letter is done correctly, you will get results. List features and benefits so they're easy to understand. Repeat your offer at least three times throughout your letter and include a call to action. Your goal is to get recipients to respond to your letter quickly and in a positive way.

Be sure to track the business generated by your direct mail campaign. By adding a response mechanism to your mailer, such as a self-addressed, stamped reply card, you can see what approach works best and build on this in future mailings. When responses start coming in, update your database with your newly acquired information.

Direct mail typically produces an average response rate of 2 to 3 percent. It doesn't seem like much, but it could give you the business edge you need to attract your next big client. What matters most is the value of the business you generate.

 ## Catch of the Day

Always follow up your mailings with a phone call. People will be more likely to remember or place you.

Keep track of your costs to establish direct mail profitability and give management hard facts about your sales and marketing results. By determining the ROI (return on investment) on your time and marketing dollars, you can justify to management that your marketing communications investment is paying off in sales and new business. If you're attracting new business and making sales, you might get a larger budget for future direct mail efforts.

A week after your mailing, take the fish by the gills, and call your prospects. Ask them if they have any questions about the information you mailed to them. Suggest a time to meet with them to discuss their needs or even to play a round of golf or go fishing. Try anything that will help you get better acquainted with your prospects and bolster your chances of working with them.

E-Mail Marketing

Online advertising often is the most cost-effective means for influencing and increasing sales results. E-mail is now touted as a highly effective marketing tool for reaching the masses, with 55 percent of U.S. households logged onto the Internet. Those who use the Internet have greater purchasing power than those who don't. Many new tools are drawing potential shoppers, including coupons, discount offers, customer targeting, and celebrity endorsements.

This high-tech form of communication appeals to salespeople because of its low cost and high leverage. Another advantage is that it usually does not require approval by a supervisor before being created and sent with the click of a mouse.

Although e-mail communication is a boon to harried salespeople looking for qualified leads, be aware of its drawbacks. It is considered impersonal and can be overlooked among other noncritical e-mails. On average, a corporate executive receives up to fifty-five e-mail messages in one day. Of those, only twenty-five are mission critical for conducting business. Your sales message can easily get lost in the crowd. That's why it's so important to target your e-mail to the recipients who will find its value relevant. It's a waste of time to send e-mail to people who have never demonstrated any interest in your product or company and have no propensity to do so.

Here are some ways to differentiate your e-mail from most others:

- Write short, snappy e-mail messages in a concise bullet point format.

- Minimize e-mail attachments to increase your chances of getting through your prospects' firewalls and to avoid clogging up their inboxes.
- Send time-sensitive e-mails with a call for action by a specified date.

There's no better way to get in front of your customers than with a free subscription to your monthly e-mail newsletter. It packs a punch by allowing you to promote recent developments in your company, offer meaningful content, and provide your business with a voice. By promising and delivering information to your subscribers each month in a nonthreatening way, you are building a trusting relationship. Focus on only servicing them in the first few months of their subscription; this will lead to sales down the road. An e-mail newsletter can be a few paragraphs describing how a customer benefited from your product or service, or a more extensive communication vehicle filled with newsworthy articles and survey data.

 ## Catch of the Day

Do not send out spam, which is unsolicited and unwanted e-mail, usually sent in bulk quantities. It's the online equivalent of the junk mail that takes up space in your mailbox. In fact, purveyors of spam can be sued in small claims court in several states, including Washington and Virginia. If your e-mail resembles spam, corporate firewalls will probably prevent it from reaching the designated recipients.

Face-to-Face Meetings
Getting face time with potential or existing customers is very effective and productive for certain product offerings.

You can build relationships with clients and also meet other influential people and key decision-makers in the organization. In a meeting, your audience feels obligated to spend time with you and is more open to discussing their needs and concerns because you've made a special trip their location. Learning their needs will help you tailor your offer and determine who the decision-makers are and who else may influence the buying decision. You may even have the opportunity to present material and demonstrate your product or offer.

Before the meeting ends, always schedule a follow-up meeting to discuss next steps. Be sure to meet and establish a rapport with the administrative assistant who will put your future calls through to your prospect.

The downside is that face-to-face meetings are very costly in terms of leverage because there are a limited number of contacts and materials that can be presented each time. The first sales meeting with a prospect can be daunting, even for professional salespeople. However, by mastering a specific set of skills and strategies, you can hone your meeting skills in no time.

Here are some ways to get the most out of your meetings:

- *Gather background information.* A prequalifying telephone call will help you to understand your prospect's wants and needs. Learn as much as possible about the company and make a list of ways it would benefit from your product or service. This means that you're selling the company what it needs, not what you want to sell.
- *Set realistic goals.* Each sales meeting moves your prospect one step closer to buying. Set your primary goal before leaving your office for the meeting. For example, your primary goal for a first meeting might be to set a date to

present a more comprehensive proposal or to provide an estimate for your work and obtain a signature to begin.

- *Prepare quality materials.* Create a set of high-quality tools for your presentations at meetings. Include everything from company business cards and general stationery to brochures, proposal documents, and presentation materials.
- *Review the materials you distribute in a sales meeting.* Scrutinize materials you intend to leave with your prospect, as they may help you close the sale. Are they well presented and well written? Do the colors, typefaces, and creative elements work together to create a memorable, professional image?

For meeting protocols and roles, revisit Chapter 3.

 **Catch of the Day**

Always follow up your face-to-face meeting with an e-mail thanking the prospects or clients for their time.

Telephone

Using the telephone to contact prospects is tricky. This method is most effective if you know who you are calling and have an established relationship with that individual. It's less effective and more intrusive if you do not. If you're familiar with your contact, this delivery method is called a phone call or conversation. If you're not, it's called telemarketing, which many salespeople jokingly refer to as "dialing for dollars."

The amount of leverage a company or sales rep can attain by using the telephone is incredible. Whether you are using a fancy dialing machine or just your fingers, a salesperson can make more contacts in one day on the phone than in

Tackle Box

> **SUCCESSFUL TELEPHONE TACTICS**
>
> - You'll get more sales by creating call lists with qualified buyers.
> - Engage the prospect in a conversation as quickly as possible.
> - Always obtain the prospect's permission to contact him or her again.
> - Schedule a follow-up call within a specified period of time, such as one week or one month.

face-to-face meetings in a whole week. To be successful, you must be scripted and efficient. Prospects are turned off by unsolicited sales calls, so you must immediately state the purpose for your call. Because your time investment is small, the likelihood of your prospect saying "no" is high. You will need to develop a thick skin to handle rejection and not be personally offended if you are dismissed before you complete your sales pitch.

Get the Meeting—One Way or Another

At a sales pipeline meeting a few years ago, I heard a creative approach to working the phone to get a face-to-face meeting. The manager indicated his team was talented but inexperienced. While good at finding opportunities, they were weaker at moving the opportunities through the funnel, which typically required a face-to-face meeting. During the sales pipeline meeting, one rep shared a large opportunity he had uncovered. This was a deal that could make or break the division's numbers. While he'd made initial contact, the rep couldn't get an appointment with the ultimate decision-maker. His many messages and e-mails had elicited no response.

Listening to the story, the sales manager grew increasingly impatient. As the rep finished up, the manager asked, "What are your plans to get a face-to-face with this decision-maker?" "I'm not sure," the rep responded. To which the manager asked, "Is there a Wal-Mart in the decision-maker's town?" Confused, the rep stammered that he didn't know. The manager shot back, "Well is there a Kmart or some sort of drugstore?" Still flustered, the rep replied he thought so. "Great," said the manager. "Get on a plane this afternoon, run by the Wal-Mart or Kmart, and pick up a toothbrush, toothpaste, and some clean underwear. Then camp out on the decision-maker's doorstep until he agrees to see you."

Everyone in the room laughed, except the manager and the rep. The manager was serious, and the rep was thinking, "This might be just the approach I need." With that, the rep left the room and made a call. Intrigued, I followed the rep.

He went to his office and called the decision-maker. When the decision-maker's secretary picked up the phone, I heard him say, "Mrs. Moore, I have a quick question for you. Is there a Wal-Mart in Melbourne, Florida?"

I could hear her response over the speakerphone; a bit baffled, she answered, "Yes." The rep responded, "I'm glad to hear that, because my manager wants me to fly down tonight in hopes of getting a quick thirty-minute meeting with Mr. Jones. Since I don't have time to run home before the next flight, I need to pick up a toothbrush, toothpaste, and some clean underwear. Can you tell me how long you think I will need to stay before I get the meeting? We know that our product will really be a nice match for your needs, and my boss will not let me leave until I get that meeting. Hopefully, it will not be too long of a wait, since I have two young kids."

With that, the secretary chuckled and said, "I can get you in for thirty minutes first thing in the morning. We need to get you home for those kids." With that he had his meeting!

Just in case your decision-maker's town doesn't have a Wal-Mart, try these ways to get an audience:

1. Use humor to break the ice and build a personal relationship.
2. Send little tokens with your product information. Don't send expensive gifts, as it will look like you are trying to buy their business.
3. Send e-mails, and follow up with phone calls. A follow-up message to a previous e-mail that breaks the ice increases the probability of a response and is not seen as a second attempt.
4. Make friends with the gatekeeper or administrative assistant. These people are more powerful than you think, and often control your decision-maker's schedule.
5. Let your quarry know you'll be in town visiting his or her peers or competitors (don't lie; schedule another meeting), and that you would like to take him or her to lunch. They will be interested in what you're doing with their contemporaries, and may feel that they are missing the boat by not speaking to you.

 ### Catch of the Day

Bottom line: Dedicate one day a week to chumming the water to increase your sales leads.

Find Time for SOV Development

When it comes to SOVs, think about what you want to accomplish, and allocate time accordingly. Plan your week around sales calls and block off a certain number of hours each week to develop and present SOVs. The amount of time you need depends on what type of SOV you are undertaking. Typically, five to ten hours per week is the norm in maintaining a continual pipeline of information.

Take ownership and create your own SOV. Whether you are the product (for example, a service provider) or you create the material and deliver the information, customers want to know that you add value and understand their needs. You make the leap from being a salesperson to a trusted adviser. This opens up a new world of opportunity for you.

How you create an SOV depends on the type of SOV you've targeted. If you want to become an expert by learning benchmarks and industry trends, gather information from people who have knowledge in these areas. Your contacts could be your existing or potential customers, the Internet, customer literature, other vendors, your competitors, customers or employees of your competitors, your network, trade journals, and competitive research firms.

CAPTAIN'S LOG

Tarpon Willie says, "If you throw out too much chum, the fish will fill up on the appetizer before you offer the main course." Know when enough's enough. The best scenario occurs when the customer has sampled your wares and asks for more.

The amount of "chum" you need depends on how much you want to sell. The amount of chum you put out should be in direct proportion to the number of buyers and decision-makers you want to contact. Remember, though, that there's a fine line between giving enough information to stimulate interest and overwhelming the client with an abundance of material. Overkill will kill the deal. Never answer all of the customer's questions. You're in the business of selling. The trick is to leave the customer wanting more by offering just the right amount of samples or literature to create awareness and a need for your product or service.

What Kind Of Business Development "Chummer" Are You?

Answer the following questions and then add your scores from each individual question to determine a total score. Match your total score to the description or category to determine what type of "Chummer" you are.

1. I enjoy people and love to understand their issues and needs.
   a. All of the time: **4 POINTS**
   b. Most of the time: **3 POINTS**
   c. When they understand my product: **1 POINT**
   d. When they understand my time is very important: **0 POINTS**
2. You know your customers, and consider them friends.
   a. Yes: **2 POINTS**
   b. No: **0 POINTS**
3. How much time do you spend developing and creating materials to stimulate interest?
   a. One day a week: **4 POINTS**
   b. More than one day a week: **2 POINTS**
   c. Less than a day a week: **1 POINT**
   d. None: **0 POINTS**

4. How much time do you spend in administrative or non-selling activities?

   a. 20%: **4 POINTS**

   b. 40%: **2 POINTS**

   c. 60%: **1 POINT**

   d. 80%: **0 POINTS**

5. How much time to you spend understanding new product offerings, trends, and issues?

   a. One hour a week: **1 POINT**

   b. One hour a day: **4 POINTS**

   c. None: **0 POINTS**

6. I plan my week before the new week starts.

   a. Agree: **2 POINTS**

   b. Disagree: **0 POINTS**

7. I rely on my company or others to send me leads.

   a. Agree: **0 POINTS**

   b. Disagree: **2 POINTS**

8. I am confident that I will meet my quota and be successful.

   a. Maybe if I am lucky: **2 POINTS**

   b. Depends on the product, my company, or marketing: **1 POINT**

   c. No: **0 POINTS**

   d. Yes: **4 POINTS**

9. Which one applies to you?

   a. I am new to this job and trying to learn: **3 POINTS**

   b. I have been around a while and know the routine: **1 POINT**

   c. I have been around a while and don't understand why things keep changing: **0 POINTS**

   d. I have been around a while but continue to leverage what I know and to develop new skills and techniques: **4 POINTS**

10. I love the challenge of developing or capturing interest in my product or my company.
  a. All of the time: **4 POINTS**
  b. Some of the time: **2 POINTS**
  c. I like others to do it and I will piggyback: **1 POINT**
  d. Just creates work and the interest is not real:
    0 POINTS
11. You understand what is expected of you in your role.
  a. Yes—all the time: **4 POINTS**
  b. Some of the time: **2 POINTS**
  c. No: **0 POINTS**

Add up your points, and read on to see what kind of business development "chummer" you are.

36–38 POINTS: TRUSTED ADVISER. You are competitive, competent, and confident and secure in your abilities. You are an expert in your field and you have status with most of your clients or customers. You love establishing new relationships. You view your clients or customers as your friends and they routinely recommend you, your company, or your products to others. You have a great system that allows you to balance creative marketing activities, selling activities, and administrative activities. You regularly develop material that stimulates customer activities. You are in the top 10 percent of sellers within your company and are frequently rewarded with extra pay, bonuses, or awards and recognition.

You should look to transfer your skills to others in order to better the organization as a whole. Continue to develop more materials and ask others to work with you. You should consider a management or a team leadership role.

30–35 POINTS: MEASURED AND RESPONSIVE. You enjoy your work and are considered a strong player. You typically work well with others and are a great team player. Many of your clients have long-term relationships with your company and have continued to maintain and grow their relationship under your management. You spend more time working with existing clients and less time establishing new clients. You effectively use material that others create. You regularly provide assistance on leads that come into the company. You have good results and typically meet your sales quota. You would like to get into the top 10 percent category. You would love to sell more and create more income for your company and yourself.

You should spend time with more "trusted advisers" and learn from their successful activities and routines. You should leverage your strong relationship management skills in order to stimulate new business. Develop an opinion regarding industry, product, or customer issues and trends.

20–29 POINTS: RELUCTANT AND UNPREPARED. Selling is a job. You are sporadically effective at it and meet your quota on an inconsistent basis. You do understand the concepts of the sales process and do use some of the available material for selling activities. You feel that your product should speak for itself and that selling is an intrusive business. You do not know your clients and have never been able to establish a relationship. Most of your business comes from others or are leads that others give you or are from pre-existing company accounts. You feel that you are underpaid and overworked and that your quota is too high.

You need to adjust your attitude and become responsible for your own success. Spend more time and effort in your profession. Develop more pride in your work and commit to learning how to develop customers and clients.

LESS THAN 20: UNMOTIVATED AND UNPRODUCTIVE. Your skills do not always match the role. You constantly have to defend your value to the organization and are not producing enough perceived value or results. The material the company has does not match your style, yet you do not create any that will. Whenever you call your customers, you have a tough time getting in the door, let alone making a sales pitch. Other salespeople seem to leave you out of the opportunities, and you feel that the company does not give you enough leads to support your quota. The product you are selling is mismatched with your opportunities. Either you need to commit yourself to development or it may be time to find a new job.

CHAPTER SEVEN

Hook 'em and Reel 'em In

NAVIGATE THE SALES PROCESS AND CLOSE THE DEAL

If you're fishing for mangrove snapper in Tampa Bay, you might try dropping anchor just off the mouth of the Little Manatee River on the shipping channel break.

One recent early morning, Tarpon Willie and I slipped into this very spot and started chumming. By the time the sun came up and the tide started to turn, we had caught close to our limit—six "keeper" size snapper. We were about to move on when a boat on the horizon caught our attention. The crew on board was causing quite a ruckus.

CAPTAIN'S LOG

"Enough with the scouting—at some point we need to fish."—Tarpon Willie

They had a large grouper on the line, and their exclamations about their "catch" pierced the morning's tranquility. "We got a Goliath," they screamed. "Biggest fish you've ever seen!"

Taking that as an invitation, we motored over to watch them reel in what likely would be the catch of the day. Three or four other boats had the same thought, and as we collectively silenced our engines, we all gazed eastward to watch this spectacle unfold. The whooping and hollering reached a crescendo—the crew was high-fiving and doing a victory dance. Skepticism crinkled Tarpon Willie's face. "If those guys don't stop jawing to us spectators and start reeling that fish in quicker, we're all going to be witness to the big one that got away."

Almost in sync with Willie's words, the line snapped and the fisherman with the pole flew backward. His line had caught the propeller of another boat. His fish was gone. Ironically, the damage had been done by a boat attracted to the crew's attention-seeking antics.

"Let that be a lesson," Tarpon Willie muttered. "Focus on getting your fish to the boat by reeling in the line and keeping the tip of the pole facing the fish. And remember, a fish ain't caught till it's caught."

It's a simple lesson, but a common mistake many novices make. Do not assign too high of a probability to a deal until you get that deal to close. Overconfidence can all too quickly turn into embarrassment—and worse, failure. While you're at it, don't waste time; move that deal through the funnel as quickly as you can. Boat anchors and propellers may lurk beneath the surface, ready to snap your line.

Understand the Sales Process

An experienced angler is attuned to subtle signals that a fish is feeding or is ready for the bait: The line starts to bob; there's a short tug on the line, or a full run on the pole. The seasoned pro knows when to engage the reel and "hit" the fish or let the fish run awhile to swallow the hook. Hooking the fish, however, is only the halfway mark to landing it. Similarly, in sales, you have to make sure you're carefully monitoring your prospect and working toward closing the deal.

A good part of this know-how comes from understanding the sales process. Chapter 1 introduced the five typical sales process steps; this chapter provides more detail. As you've likely encountered, each step has many moving parts, but to keep it simple, I'm focusing on core components and activities of a standard sales process.

As explained in the following sections, each step in the sales process has different attributes and requires different behaviors in order to move the transaction into the next stage, and, ultimately, conclude with an agreement to buy.

Step #1: Identify

This step is sometimes called "above the funnel" work. The focus is on finding a potential customer with an interest, need, or desire for your product or service. Your prospect may be well aware of the need, or as yet completely unaware, awaiting the right SOV or pitch to bait the hook.

CAPTAIN'S LOG
Tarpon Willie explains fishing simply by saying, "You look for fish (Identify); you study the tides and times (Qualify); you throw out your bait (Propose); you hook 'em and reel 'em in (Close); and then you clean and eat 'em (Fulfill)." Pretty similar to selling—the same logic applies.

Your role is to uncover that need, interest, or desire; bring it to the surface; and determine how you can meet it. Factors to consider in identifying prospects include the following:

- Have they purchased before?
- Do they have an issue you can help resolve?
- Are they reading literature or showing up at events that previous purchasers read or attended?
- Do they use a competitor's products or services?

If any of the above signals surface, chances are you stand the chance of getting a nibble.

Step #2: Qualify

In step two, you are qualifying; that is, assessing your identified prospect's true potential to purchase your product or service. In other words, you need to determine whether prospects will take the BAIT:

- Do they have the budget to purchase your offer?
- Do they have the authority to make the purchase?
- Do they have a strong interest in your offer and in pursuing the sales process?
- Is the timing appropriate? When do you predict a purchase might occur?

If it looks like your prospect will take the BAIT, the waters may be right to jump in with your proposal. For more about BAIT, see Chapter 1.

Step #3: Propose

At this stage, your deal becomes real. The focus is on presenting the benefits, features, and abilities of your product or service. You must confirm the terms and conditions of an opportunity to make sure your proposition is attractive and directionally correct.

Proposal activities include the following:

- Presentation and/or demonstration that proposes a solution with pricing
- Agreement that an offer or request is coming
- Verbal offer (may be trial balloon to gauge the prospect's true desire)
- Formal communications via a verbal commitment or formal written document

If you've moved into the proposal stage, you have a good chance of reeling in your catch.

Step #4: Close

In this step, your prospect becomes your customer. As Tarpon Willie would say, "This is where ya boat da fish." The focus is on culminating your activities with an agreement to become partners. You agree to provide a product or service and your customer agrees to compensate you for it. Activities include:

- Negotiating the pricing, volume, timing, or any miscellaneous terms and conditions of your sale
- Resolving objections
- Formalizing an agreement to move forward

At this stage, you may be ready to savor your catch, but if you don't properly manage the final step—fulfillment—you may be buying take-out instead.

Step #5: Fulfill

Many business developers and business leaders, including myself, would argue that fulfillment is the most important step. Yet others will claim that fulfillment is the role of an employee who's not earning commissions or incentives. To settle the argument, I went to the source—an American dictionary, which defines a sale as "the exchanging of goods and services for an agreed amount of money." The key words here are "exchanging" and "agreed." In my eyes, exchanging and agreeing to terms for goods or services are akin to fulfilling. If either party fails to meet his or her commitment, there is no deal, and the "sale" can vanish as quickly as a silver mullet slipping out of that hole in your net. Stay as involved as is reasonably possible in the entire sales process, and keep tabs on fulfillment to make sure your customers get what they paid for.

In fulfillment, the focus is on providing the value promised to your customer. Activities include:

- Product or service delivery
- Account management
- Sales support
- Technical support

Don't let your customer become "the big one that got away" because his or her needs weren't met during fulfillment and delivery.

Assess the Probability of Your Sale

Tarpon Willie says, "You can't cook 'em till you catch 'em. So don't plan your fish fry before your fishing trip, or you might be eatin' a chicken dinner."

How real is your deal? This is the million-dollar question many sales organizations struggle to answer. Companies have sprung up throughout the sales industry offering sophisticated software tools to help sales organizations and salespeople figure out how to accurately forecast their sales yield.

Your sales yield is a probability-adjusted figure that looks at all prospects in your sales funnel or pipeline, and calculates a total dollar amount based upon your prospects' stage in the sales process. For example, if you have a $1,000 opportunity that is in the proposal stage and has a 50 percent likelihood of closing, your yield on this deal would be $500. If you then move the opportunity to the closing stage, which has an 85 percent chance of closing, the yield would be $850. Your total yield would be the sum of all of the deals in each stage.

 Catch of the Day

Use your sales funnel to help manage your day-to-day interactions and decide whether you need to "troll" for more business or focus on closing what's in your net. It can mean the difference between making quota or missing it.

As a sales rep, understanding your yield helps you forecast what your week, month, quarter, or year is looking like. You can gauge how close you are coming to your targets. If your probability-adjusted yield is $50,000 for the quarter and your quota is $75,000, then you either need to find more deals, or increase the odds of closing your existing deals.

So what are the typical probabilities of deals in each step of the sales process? Some general probabilities are shown in the following table. In reviewing the table, keep in mind that every sales process or deal can be different. Some steps can be skipped or conducted all on one sales call or phone call, while others may last months and require multiple interactions. Also, the number of deals decreases as you progress through the funnel—some qualify; others vaporize. This is a good thing because as you propose and close, you want to be juggling fewer deals that hold higher probability. Don't waste time on deals that have a low probability of closing. Hence the term "funnel"—larger at the top so more goes in, but narrower on the bottom so fewer pass through and fall into the mix.

What's the Probability of Your Deal?

Step	Typical Probability	What's It All Mean?
Identify	10%–20%	Deal has been identified, but not yet qualified. Buyer has a low probability of closing. Typically, each deal in this stage of the funnel has a 10%–20% chance of closing. Depending upon your product or your sales process, the odds can be lower or higher. For example, an inbound call center role might have greater odds and might close in one call; thus, the probability at the onset is much greater. In some cases, you might close immediately.
Qualify	20%–40%	Deal is now qualified. The buyer has indicated his or her intention and is considering a purchase. These deals typically have a 20%–40% chance of closing. Many sales process and probability percentages start at this stage. Some companies and salespeople feel that until a company indicates its intentions, an opportunity is not legitimate.
Propose	40%–60%	You are about to propose formally or informally. Depending upon the formality, the range can be from 40% to 60%. This is where the odds may start to really tip in your favor—unless, of course, five or six companies are proposing. Some companies believe that if a proposal is written, their odds can be even greater than the 40%–60% indicated here. Whatever the case for your organization, the more you are proposing on deals, the more you are closing on deals.

Close	60%–80%	Depending on how you define your closing stage, your probabilities will vary. In some companies, the closing stage means the deal is won. In others, this stage is a process and the deal is not closed until you actually ship it, or you receive payment. Either way, your probabilities have increased, while your deal flow at this stage has decreased.
Fulfill	80%–100%	In many cases, as discussed earlier, a deal is not won until you meet your end of the agreement. Until you have fully shipped, delivered, processed, and so on, your deal has a chance of being canceled. Although this is the last step in the funnel, many companies have a payment-received step, stipulating that until they receive payment, the deal is not finalized or counted toward sales rep commissions.

Spot the Signs of Someone Ready to Purchase

"Was that a fish?" Tarpon Willie can hear a flip of a tail, a strike at the surface, or pelicans diving on bait from a mile away. It doesn't matter if the motor is running or the river's fogged in. He's always on the lookout for the tell-"tail" signs that fish are in the area and ready to feed. He's an expert at spotting the signs that signal it's time to fish. Customers may send out equally subtle clues. Reps need to "look for the tail" and move in to make the sale.

THIS AIN'T NO FISH TALE!

Recently, I had the chance to sit in on quarterly reviews at a large consumer products company. On the hot seat was the designated top performer for the past eighteen months. The topic was quota attainment and account planning. This rep had been with the company for six years, yet prior to these last eighteen months, she had never consistently met her quota. In fact, three years ago, she had been on a performance improvement plan and was slated for termination if her results didn't improve.

Discussing her sales approach, the rep espoused a sound sales process, but I heard nothing that indicated she had found the "secret bait" or "magic lure." Her territory hadn't changed, nor had her manager. She had no new products to sell, and she hadn't taken any training. I learned that eighteen months prior, the company had installed a new sales force automation (SFA) tool. The software came equipped with a funnel and forecasting tool that allowed reps to chart deals and track their status against quota throughout the operating period. The rep acknowledged that she used the tool religiously. "I figure out how many deals I need to generate, how many I need to close, and when I should push more aggressively to meet my target. I can see how adding deals into the funnel affects my compensation. For instance, I need ten prospects to equal one deal. It is simple math."

This rep had figured out how to manage her sales process and deal flow to maximize her results. She wasn't working harder or logging longer hours. Her success stemmed from her understanding of adjusted probabilities. She'd become a top rep by reviewing her sales pipeline, calculating her yield, and charting her sales strategy accordingly.

Knowing how to recognize the signals in sales is one of the first skills you need to develop if you want to rank among the top sellers in your organization. These skills help you understand whether you need to speed up, slow down, continue in process, or hoist anchor and end your pursuit. Whether your sales process is long in duration and requires many personal visits or consists of short, transactional phone conversations, always keep your eyes and ears open.

 Tackle Box

Tackle Box

QUESTIONS TO HELP YOU MOVE THROUGH THE PROCESS MORE QUICKLY

- What time can I come by to bring you a sample? This line of questioning helps set up the next meeting.

- If you were to make a choice today, how would you pick up your purchase? This line of questioning helps your prospect to think about owning your product.

- How often did you plan on using the item? This line of questioning helps your prospect to think about how he or she would use your product.

- Is your staff or family excited [about the product]? This line of questioning will help your prospect think through how others will react to the purchase.

- How will you pay or finance this transaction when you get to that point? This line of questioning will help your prospect think through the financial commitments.

Understanding and being able to spot the signals of a buyer ready to purchase can save you and your prospect many hours of effort, time, and money. Look for the following verbal and behavioral cues from your prospects—they can signal a sale on the horizon:

Asking product questions. Whenever prospects inquire about your product or service, they show interest. Depending on the amount of detail you've provided so far, product questions can signal how ready a prospect is to buy. If the questions are relevant and consistent with those you've heard in prior successful deals, chances are you have a strong candidate who's ready to move to the next step. The questions might be simple inquiries about product color, setup time, or your shipping schedules, yet they indicate interest and show the prospect cares. If prospects lack interest, they won't ask.

 ### Catch of the Day

The signs of a sale can be as subtle as a customer asking, "How easy would it be to set up your product?" or as direct as, "When can you send me a contract?" Signals can come in the form of verbal dialogue, written communications, physical body language, or different behaviors or mannerisms. The key is to recognize the client's desire to move forward and then provide the proper information to progress him or her toward the next step.

Requesting company information. Questions about who you represent, what you do, and/or what your company does signal a desire to proceed, as long as you and your company are credible.

Probing for more detail. A prospect that wants more details is one who has heard, seen, or read something that has identified, and potentially qualified, need or desire for your product or service. A desire for more facts and features signals that your prospect wants to fully investigate the potential of buying what you have to sell.

Inviting others to join. When prospects invite colleagues to join the conversation, the meeting, or even the e-mail distribution chain, they are seeking acceptance to continue the sales process with you. They would not devote their time, or the time of others, unless they have a clear interest in moving forward. Be aware, however, that in some cases, they might be looking for approval to dump you. Make sure you've spotted the signs and correctly interpreted them prior to this meeting.

CAPTAIN'S LOG

Tarpon Willie says, "Once you eat a snook, you're always hooked. No other fish fights as hard or tastes as good—you always want more." Design your demo to pass the snook taste test.

Wanting a product demo. Any prospect that asks to touch, feel, meet, greet, taste, or use your product wants to experience the benefits that come with a purchase. At this point, you've moved beyond cognitive evaluation; you've entered emotional decision-making territory. Once a prospect gets a feel for "new or better," it's hard to go back to the old way of doing business. Think about taking a new car for a test drive. In your mind, you may "only be looking." Yet once you smell that new-car aroma and press your foot to the accelerator, your old car seems woefully inadequate. You're mentally sold on acquiring a car that's fresh, clean, and current. If you don't buy the car that day, you will soon. You're hooked!

Asking for the terms, aka "putting it in writing." Bingo. When a prospect asks for terms or asks you to put your discussions in writing, it indicates desire to formalize your deal or substantiate your intentions to serve the company. The prospect is nearing a decision and wants to confirm that he or she has heard you correctly.

Requesting references. This request may start the sales process, allowing the prospect to qualify you as a suitable partner. It also can occur near the end, helping the prospect confirm the purchase through affirmation. Whatever the timing, asking for references signals readiness to move forward. Handle those references properly. Don't lose the deal because your reference isn't prepared.

Exuding a relaxed, unhurried demeanor. Body language and mannerisms can signal the need to move more quickly or ease up and slow down your presentation. A client who is calm, relaxed, and engaged shows it through open posture and an inviting smile or greeting. That client is open to your offer.

Complimenting you, your process, or your product. Compliments from prospects signal encouragement to continue on the same path and an invitation to tell them more. Even if the prospects aren't ready to purchase, they like what they're hearing and are willing to listen to more. Keep going—but also be careful! Make sure the positive response is genuine and not just a way of letting you down gently. I've encountered buyers who did not feel comfortable giving a simple "no," and instead loaded on the compliments. Then, just when the sales team started to hit the reel, the client snapped the line, and swam away.

Showing up. A prospect that "shows up"—via a phone call, meeting request, browsing your show room, or asking for your opinion—has some sort of need. Such prospects have "surfaced" and are looking for reasons to stay above the water. Keep them afloat!

Take Advantage of a High Tide

In a high tide, all boats rise and a lot more fish are in the water. When it's "high tide" with your prospect, you're well positioned to make the sale and close the deal. If you spot these high-tide behaviors, chances are, your prospect is willing to take your bait:

- Smiles and engages in conversation
- Appears poised and confident with your presence
- Meets you at the elevator
- Seems to be waiting for your call
- Is on time and prepared for the discussion
- Gives you undivided attention and is unwilling to be distracted

While these signals are positive, don't get overconfident and start showboating, like the party-boat "anglers" mentioned at the start of this chapter. Until you have a firm commitment and you are fulfilling the customer's expectations, never allow any slack in your lines. Keep your discipline and professionalism throughout all stages of the sales process. Remember, your goal is a happy customer. Until you have completed the transaction—and have clear evidence that your customer is happy—you have not completed the job. As Tarpon Willie says, "Keep dem lines tight."

Keep Your Momentum Going

In sales, less successful reps often spend an inordinate amount of time prepping, but leave no time for selling and closing the deal. High performers, on the other hand, crave the hunt; they keep trying different approaches and always ask for the sale.

The following statements and questions are the equivalent of putting your lines in the water—they can help move your deal through the sales process and determine where you stand:

- Let's confirm our discussion.
- Can I put our conversation in writing?
- Can we confirm the next date (put the date on the calendar)?
- Should we get others (for example, the boss) involved?
- Can I put the parameters or outline of our deal in writing?
- What's your time frame for making a decision?
- Are there any other options you would like to discuss?
- Can I allocate or hold a product for you?
- Can I take your order?

Beware a Low Tide

In a low tide, there's usually less water, which means fewer fish, and therefore less opportunity to make a catch. Take the following low-tide behaviors as warning signs that your prospect may be swimming out to sea.

Glances at a watch or clock. This is a sign to hurry up. Prospects who do this either have heard enough and want you to move on, or they want you out of their office. Tactfully inquire as to how much time you have. When you learn the scheduled end time, mention that you can speed it up if they would like you to. Show that you are sensitive to their schedule and can be flexible.

CAPTAIN'S LOG

Tarpon Willie reminds me that "things aren't perfect all the time." When fishing, you can plan and prepare, but even so, you still face uncertain conditions and the potential for human error. At some point, you have to take your best guess, put your lines in the water, and go for the sale.

THIS AIN'T NO FISH TALE!

My first sales manager, a great storyteller, believed that mistakes are often the best teachers. Early in his career, my manager was paired with a top seller. When his partner left the company, my manager acquired the accounts, one of which was the firm's top account. The customer provided a steady revenue stream and also made a couple of additional big purchases each year. My manager grew the revenue stream, but after eighteen months, hadn't gotten the big deal. In pursuit of this sale, he reworked his account plans, analyzed his targeting, engaged in more above-the-funnel work, and arranged various meetings. Yet the company wasn't buying the big product. Chalking it up to a relationship issue, my manager's VP of sales met with the customer to review their long association. The VP of sales mentioned to the customer that the traditional big purchase hadn't been made in the past two years. He asked whether some issue had cropped up. Dumbfounded, the customer declared that the only "issue" was that no one had asked him to make the purchase. He'd concluded that the company had retired the product, and was now buying it from a competitor.

My sales manager never made that mistake again, nor did the sales teams he came to manage. He made it clear to every sales rep that at some point, you have to put the line in the water and ask for the sale.

Flips through the presentation; appears uninterested. Somehow, you are missing these prospects' point of interest, or they are not getting yours. Subtly ask if they would like to change directions, or flip to the "ah-ha" (the key message of your presentation). Don't embarrass the clients or imply that you have observed that they seem distracted or impatient. Inquire in a way that helps your prospects get what they need out of the demonstration or presentation. Your focus should be on your prospect, not on getting the attention back to you or your positioning.

Shows impatience: Your prospect gets up from the desk, reads e-mails, taps hands or feet, ruffles through other papers. These are clear signals that either your presentation is missing something that is important to your client, or your client is no longer engaged. A couple of tactics to employ:

1. Stop your presentation and ask if the client needs some time to attend to unfinished business. If you get an apology, chalk the behavior up to a momentary distraction, and move on. If the client continues without comment, your deal is probably in big trouble.

2. Try to engage the prospect: Ask for questions or comment. Inquire as to his or her reaction to what you've discussed so far. Determine whether the client wants to focus in on something specific.

The key is to get the prospect focused once again, not to lose control of your presentation. Be sure to get all of your key points on the table as you also address the client's issues and points of interest.

Takes phone calls. In most cases, this is the strongest signal that interest has waned. You may still be safe if your prospect fields just one call with apologies before and after. More than one call, and you are in big trouble. You might try to motion your willingness to step out of the office until the phone call ends. If a prospect is interested in you and your offer, he or she will be embarrassed and motion you to stay, rushing to finish the call. If the client nods "yes," step outside, and then suggest rescheduling.

Provides short answers to questions that merit more than a "yes" or "no." Short replies to icebreaker questions ("How's the weather been in LA the last few days?" or "Do your pursue any hobbies in your off-hours?") that are meant to open things up can actually shut things down and fill the room with unease. Quickly move on to strategic questions, since they may not have time for idle chat. If the client answers the more important, strategic questions with only "yes" or "no," that is not a good sign. Allow clients to talk or ask questions so they get a chance to steer the boat.

Answers your questions with questions. This is one of my personal favorites. If you ask a prospect, "Would you like to discuss how my product can help?" and he or she responds, "Would you like to discuss how your product can help?" you might be in trouble! Unless your prospect is also training to be a therapist, he or she may be playing games with you. Try answering questions confidently, with poise and professionalism; you may win the client over. On a ride-along, I heard a sales rep reply, "Oh yes, I would like to discuss how my product can help. I think you'll be pleasantly surprised at how quickly I can tell you and cite examples. May I please try?" The client was disarmed by the rep's response and could only say "yes."

> **CAPTAIN'S LOG**
>
> *Tarpon Willie says, "If someone can guide my boat to a better spot that will catch us more fish, then here's the wheel."* It's okay to let your prospect drive the meeting; just be prepared for whatever direction it may take.

In trying to reverse troublesome behaviors, mannerisms, or interferences during your meeting, be careful not to offend. The goal is to create harmony and trust. Never show frustration, or worse, annoy or embarrass your prospect. Figure out why he or she might be sending negative signs and behave accordingly.

Signs That It May Be Time to Pull Up Anchor

Whether business or personal, relationships often follow the same patterns. Think back to a time when someone broke your heart. You knew something wasn't right, but you couldn't put your finger on it. The signals were little things: less interest, less time, strange comments, reluctance to discuss the future. Clients send out these signals, too. Watch for these "breakup" signs; they could be early indicators that your client is ready to move on.

- Your prospect starts asking lots of tough questions that have no clear answers.
- Your prospect observes that your competitors will be "tough to beat."
- Your prospect compliments other vendors that have done "lots of work with us."
- Your prospect mentions that company policy dictates three competitive bids—and then your meetings or conversations dwindle or disappear beyond the horizon.

Overcome Objections or Face Rejection

If the fish spits the hook or takes the fisherman down to the rocks, it's time to change strategy. Perhaps you need bigger hooks or heavier tackle. Lack of bites may be a sign of "fishing on credit"; in other words, there's no bait on the line. Or perhaps the fish has taken the bait but not the hook. Giving up is not the answer. If the customer doesn't nibble, it may be time to underscore the product benefits or value proposition, or switch products altogether. "A" players never panic, become overly aggressive, or doubt their skills. They work harder to determine their prospects' needs and repackage the product to dissolve customer reservations.

If objections to your pitch surface, believe it or not, you're in a good position. To get this far—and indeed, to get a response—you've done many things right. You have gone to the right spot, chummed the water, and hooked the fish; now you're trying to reel it in. If there was no interest, you never would be in this conversation. Stay positive. Overcoming objections is part of the sales process; it's the challenge that makes the win sweet! Few astute buyers purchase on the first pitch or offer, and they rarely buy with the first pricing proposal. If you face objections, respond and react based upon the concerns.

In some cases, you can't overcome objections and you will inevitably face rejection. Rejection is never fun, but is part of sales. The most successful sales reps understand this and move on quickly.

Use these tips to help handle rejection:

CAPTAIN'S LOG
Tarpon Willie says, "If you've never lost a fish, you're spending too much time on the dock!" Even the best have had some sure things slip away. Remind yourself that there are many more opportunities; you can't sell them all. Have a thick skin.

- Use lost opportunities as a chance to learn and grow. Take a lost opportunity personally—it's the best way to motivate and force yourself to learn and develop.
- Do a post-deal analysis, outlining the areas that might have caused your downfall. Make a commitment to improve.

- Discuss the decisions with your customer and let him or her know you are happy to provide guidance or assistance in the future, even if the customer went with your competitor.
- Discuss the loss with your sales team. Seek input from other reps and your manager. You likely will find that they have faced similar losses and can share the ways they've overcome objections or repositioned their approach to meet the next opportunity better.

Tarpon Willie often says, "If the fish aren't lovin' you, then don't waste time trying to love 'em back. Move on to the ones that will!" It's the same with customers. Sometimes, even your best efforts still won't get you the sale. Better to turn your attention to other prospects.

Address Buyer's Remorse Before It Has a Chance to Surface

Make sure your sale stays in the boat or makes it back to the dock. Just as anglers might second-guess the fish that put them over the limit, buyers may have doubts once the deal is sealed. These doubts are commonly referred to as buyer's remorse—best defined as customers feeling regret about their purchase or second-guessing the reason why they made the commitment in the first place. Remorse is common for many purchases, even very small ones.

To help overcome buyer's remorse (you can never really avoid it), continually reinforce your buyers' decisions to purchase your product or service. Reconfirm the value a prospect will receive from the choice. Remind the customer of the benefits. Emphasize that the benefits will far outweigh

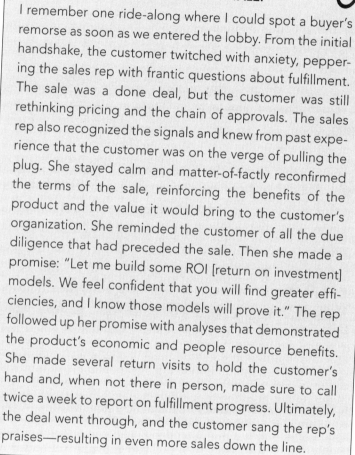

THIS AIN'T NO FISH TALE!

I remember one ride-along where I could spot a buyer's remorse as soon as we entered the lobby. From the initial handshake, the customer twitched with anxiety, peppering the sales rep with frantic questions about fulfillment. The sale was a done deal, but the customer was still rethinking pricing and the chain of approvals. The sales rep also recognized the signals and knew from past experience that the customer was on the verge of pulling the plug. She stayed calm and matter-of-factly reconfirmed the terms of the sale, reinforcing the benefits of the product and the value it would bring to the customer's organization. She reminded the customer of all the due diligence that had preceded the sale. Then she made a promise: "Let me build some ROI [return on investment] models. We feel confident that you will find greater efficiencies, and I know those models will prove it." The rep followed up her promise with analyses that demonstrated the product's economic and people resource benefits. She made several return visits to hold the customer's hand and, when not there in person, made sure to call twice a week to report on fulfillment progress. Ultimately, the deal went through, and the customer sang the rep's praises—resulting in even more sales down the line.

any risk associated with the purchase. Apply these methods to anticipate and head off buyer's remorse:

1. Confirm that your customers went through the decision-making process armed with all the important data needed to make a smart decision.

2. Reinforce the reasons they made the purchase. Reiterate comments they made during the process that led them to the sale.

3. Deliver the product on time, on budget, and/or to the terms of your agreement. Don't make them regret you or your company!

4. Remind them of the benefits and/or efficiencies they will receive from their decision. Make the purchase real by helping them visualize and savor the value.

Once you've closed the deal, aim to deliver as soon as possible. The time between signing and delivery is the most critical. The longer the delay, the more time the client has to back away. Fill the time with logistics, and skillfully redirect any uneasy comments about the price. As Tarpon Willie says, "Just when you think you've tired the fight out of your fish, it can get spooked by the sight of your boat and take off again. You've got to turn that fish around so it's easier to bring it into the boat. Stay close in the final moments, and always be ready for that last fight."

Turn the Fish Around: What Do You Say When . . .?

At every stage of the sales process, you must be prepared to move your prospect from unease to "at ease." Sometimes a thoughtful question is all that's required. Just as you can't land a trout with a shark hook, you won't assuage a customer's concern with an overly aggressive response.

Take this short quiz to find out how well you can respond to customers' concerns. Match each of these customer statements with the best sales rep's response from the list that follows.

Customer Statements:

1. You've *identified* your prospect, but in the first conversation he or she says, "I haven't figured out how serious I am and if I have any budget. I need to gather my thoughts and think through what I might need or not need."

You say: _____. (Choose A, B, C, D, E, F, G, H, or I.)

2. You have a *qualified* prospect on the line, but then he or she hits you with, "I don't know if I can make the decision on this."

Your response is: _____.

3. Just when you're ready to *propose*, the customer backs away, saying: "This is going to be too much money and take too much time for me to get involved."

You put a smile on your face and say: _____.

4. You think you've *closed* the deal, when your client replies, "This looks interesting. But I cannot make a decision on this at this time."

You take a deep breath and respond: _____.

5. The sale is signed, sealed, but not delivered. You're overseeing *fulfillment* when your customer calls and says, "I am not sure I really need this. I want to reconsider my options."

You say: _____.

Sales Rep's Response:

A. "What issue is slowing your decision? Is there something that you heard or saw that concerns you? Maybe I can help you think through those concerns or issues."

B. "Let me once again explain all the benefits of this product. Maybe you were not listening the first time. Do you have time to listen now?"

C. "What are the major or key questions that you will ask yourself to better identify your needs and understand your budget requirements? Can I help you think them through?"

D. "I think you're making a big mistake. This product could lend great efficiency to your organization, and we all know that's a huge problem for you."

E. "I know this was an important and critical decision for you and your organization. Rest assured, you have looked at this from many angles, and I am confident that you have fully thought this through, and have made a fine choice."

F. "I can't believe I'm hearing this. After all the conversations we've had, you can't back away now."

G. "You might be surprised. I am happy to put some material together that details how we might help you and what it might cost. Would that be helpful for you?"

H. "I know this can be a tough decision. You might consider pulling others in to get their opinion. I am happy to discuss this option with anyone else. Would you like me to help set up those discussions?"

I. "I'm going to pretend you didn't say that. Instead, I'm going to hang up and let you sleep on it."

THE RIGHT ANSWERS ARE:
1-C; 2-H; 3-G; 4-A; 5-E

If you even thought about matching B, D, F, or I, go back to Chapter 1, start reading, and keep going!

CHAPTER EIGHT

Catch Some More!

MANAGE THE ACCOUNT AND MAXIMIZE ITS POTENTIAL

One morning as I arrived at the dock for a day of fishing, I overheard Tarpon Willie on the "horn" with a fishing buddy. He was getting the lowdown on where the fish were congregating and what baits they were hitting. After he hung up, he opened a tackle box and pulled out a couple of fancy new lures. He then selected tackle from another newly acquired, space-saving, space-age tackle repository. With his lures and tackle at the ready, he set his satellite-guided fish finder and we headed off to see the fish.

CAPTAIN'S LOG
"One fish does not make the day."
—Tarpon Willie

I asked Willie how he stayed current on all the gear and equipment that he used. "Well, son," he replied, "I read the magazines and watch all the fishing shows, but the best source is the local marina. Jack, the store manager, is the most experienced and trustworthy guy around. I've bought three boats from him. He's the source for my bait and all my tackle. And I've met most of my fishing buddies in that place too. I give Jack all my business. You know, we started our relationship as salesman and customer, but now we are good friends. He has taught me a lot, as I have him. He's a trusted fishing partner!"

Do your customers consider you a trusted partner? You better make sure they do. It's easier to sell to an existing customer (working from an established relationship) than to start fresh with someone new. People do business with people they trust, so it's up to you to leverage the opportunities that come your way into a continual source of sales. That's the first step in wise account management.

 Catch of the Day

Account management is best defined as a "go-to-market" approach that allows an organization to build credibility, trust, and thought leadership to a high-potential or high-value account through a positive and mutually beneficial relationship.

Manage Accounts to Get the Most Potential

You can leverage a low-impact sale through good account management and relationship building to get more sales, bigger orders, or more attractive opportunities. Given the increasingly complex business conditions and competition for time, attention, and budgetary dollars, learning to sell through great account management is becoming a required skill. In many cases, customers want to establish a relationship for long-term purchasing decisions.

Some customer relationships lend themselves more readily to account management, but all jobs present opportunities to sell more somewhere down the line. As shown in the following chart, there are five types of sales, which fall into three categories: Penetration, Acquisition, and Retention. Proper account management typically covers penetration and retention sales. Yet acquisition sellers, who apply the skills of good account management to their selling situation, can create openings to find new sales and extend relationships.

CURRENT OFFERINGS	NEW OFFERINGS		
Buyer Penetration (Additional Buying Points or Usage)	Product Penetration (New Products to Current/New Users)	P}	Penetration Selling
Account Acquisition (Current Products to New Accounts)	Market Acquisition (New Products to New Accounts)	A}	Acquisition Selling
Retention		R}	Maintenance / Renewal Selling

Let's take a look at each of these types of selling in more detail:

Penetration Sales

BUYER PENETRATION: Buyer penetration is about selling more of the same product to the same customer. It's catching the same fish you've hooked before, with the same bait, and in the same spot. Good account management breeds buyer penetration. This type of sale is generally short and most efficient simply because you have done it before and the customer knows you. This is not to imply that the sale is easy or simple. Success comes when you maintain a high level of quality, continually introduce new applications for your product, or keep adding value for your clients. If you don't maintain superior quality and professionalism, your client may snap the line and swim away.

PRODUCT PENETRATION: You're in a new spot, with new bait, but you're trying to lure the same type of fish. Product penetration is selling new products to existing customers or new users within the same company. This type of sale is also a key output of good account management. It's probably the best place to be in terms of selling: You have access to your core products, but also get to offer your existing customers some new products, keeping your value fresh. Penetrating accounts to sell more products can be the most profitable type of sale. Selling costs are likely lower (you're already there and generally, don't have to maneuver the qualification stage). It's typically a quicker sale, too.

Acquisition Sales

MARKET ACQUISITION: Clearly, this is the toughest type of sale. You're always selling new products to new customers. It's like looking for new fish, in unfamiliar water, and trying to entice them with a new lure or bait that you've never used before. Every day you face a new customer and have to introduce yourself, your company, and your product—and after every sale, you start all over again with a new prospect. In most cases, your sales cycle is longer and more tedious. Your product is new; therefore, you have limited history or experience with it. In addition, your customer doesn't know you. Tarpon Willie would say, "Your chances are a lot lower 'cause you're fishing in unfamiliar waters with a new jig."

ACCOUNT ACQUISITION: In this case, you're looking for a new fish, in a new spot, but you can rely on your favorite jig to attract some attention. Your customer is always new but you're selling products with a history and, therefore, can leverage experiences or examples. You still have to sell to

THIS AIN'T NO FISH TALE

Successful reps know how to maximize account potential. While interviewing reps to assess sales-force effectiveness in a client company, I was struck by the demeanor of one rep identified by her management as a star producer. While polite, helpful, and generous with her responses, she clearly was rushed and seemingly impatient to be elsewhere. When I shared my observation, she explained that she put an ROI (return on investment) to everything she did during the day. The interview, while important, was using the time she reserved for talking with customers. "There's a high correlation between time spent with customers and time spent generating sales," she advised me. "In the first half of the week, I spend 60 percent of my time with three to five existing customers. Every time I do that, an opportunity or two will come my way. The next two days, I do the reverse—focus 60 percent of the time on prospects, and 40 percent on my existing client base, which I'm always trying to penetrate."

That same day, I also interviewed a "B" player, who arrived thirty minutes early and clearly was in no hurry to leave. When asked about his sales process, he replied that he devoted 60 to 70 percent of his time to prospecting new accounts. Both reps had the same number of accounts, but given the relationship nature of the business, the first rep was clearly the winner. She placed a premium on maximizing current accounts and she got the sales results she was seeking.

new customers, so your introduction is of key importance, but at least you're not starting from square one each time. You're familiar with your product and often acquainted with your prospect. Tarpon Willie would say, "Your chances have improved, but you don't know what type of fish is swimming below the surface and if they will hit your jig."

Retention Sales

Retention sales occur when your customer renews current contracts. Retention hinges on solid account management—building trust with the customer, continually adding value, and keeping your favorite fishing spot unpolluted and undiscovered.

 Catch of the Day

If you're not getting sufficient carry-on sales from your existing accounts, maybe your account management capabilities are not up to par. Look at the account management competencies ("Do You Have What It Takes to Catch Some More?") at the end of this chapter to figure out which skills, abilities, and behaviors you need to acquire or perfect.

Apply the Principles of Proper Account Management

Consider the value of effective account management:

- Increased sales—Customers who know you will buy more from you.
- Leads—Customers who know you have a higher probability of sending leads your way.
- Cost—It is cheaper to sell to existing customers than new ones.

- Time—It generally takes less time to sell to existing customers. They know what you bring to the table.

Proper account management starts with understanding who your client is and how he or she would like to be served; it culminates in trust and respect. A sales rep who can demonstrate these qualities will be able to call that client a "friend" and will likely enjoy a long-term relationship that will produce a great catch for many years. The following basic principles will help you provide real value to your customer.

Build a contact list and organization chart to understand the key players. Identify all key buyers, coaches, and other key relationships (such as next-generation leaders) within the client organization. Once you develop it, keep the list current. Organizational changes happen often. Don't lose your contacts or position because you don't know the organization. Make sure that you schedule these individuals for regular calls to keep in touch.

Thoroughly understand a client's business. Account management is *not* about selling, moving on, and making a call or two each month. It's about studying the business and learning what does and does not make your client effective. Knowing the business enables you to spot deficiencies in a customer's operations (for example, failure to use latest technologies). This "delta" or gap can create a sales opportunity—providing you're equipped with the expertise or product to close the gap. Know your customer's industry, the hot trends, and their customers' issues!

As an example of the importance of knowing your client's business, consider the following story:

Out covering his territory, a sales rep made a pit stop at a customer's site. He wasn't actively selling, just managing his account, and ensuring that the customer was happy with their partnership. Walking through the warehouse with his customer, the rep noticed that the small company's storage procedures did not maximize the space. He asked his contact if they could pay a visit to the warehouse supervisor. Once in the supervisor's office, the rep suggested a way to reconfigure boxes and create more space. He apologized if he was speaking out of turn, but explained that he worked with other customers whose warehouses had grown over time. Over the years, he'd taken notice of the efficiencies employed to make the most of limited storage. The supervisor responded that he welcomed the rep's observations. "That's why we work with your company. Not only do you provide a great product, you give us helpful tips that add value to our growing company. We want to grow too, and we like that you know the business."

CAPTAIN'S LOG

Tarpon Willie says, "Don't overfish a spot." Whether with fish or customers, focus on opportunities for impact or those that fit your strategy. Don't try to sell a client anything or everything. Be selective. As hard as it might be, sometimes you have to turn down low-impact or nonconforming opportunities.

Spend time with your clients. Invest in the relationship through continual touch-points and substantive time on-site. If your job, distance, or budget makes face time difficult to arrange, you can still make phone calls and be proactive. The more time you spend with the customer after the sale, the more you demonstrate how much you value the relationship.

Extend key relationships: Continually expand your relationships across your customer's organization. Don't stop with your main contact, or with the particular organization; keep expanding and meeting people. You never know when an organizational change may occur.

THIS AIN'T NO FISH TALE!

My first sales manager taught me the art of selling, which is to avoid being perceived as selling. People don't like to be sold to, but generally, they like to purchase. If accounts are buying from you, make sure they are happy with what they have. If they have additional needs or issues, be there for them. Inevitably, providing this level of service will generate more revenue and assure long-term relationships. This message didn't stick until I tagged along on a sales call with an overly aggressive sales rep who would not stop selling. Relatively inexperienced, this rep had a set of hot accounts—also known as "gimmies"—that were meant to get her started in the business. Visiting the head of purchasing in one of these accounts, the rep was insistent in her tone and demeanor. She used phrases such as, "What would you like to order?" "You haven't bought anything lately." "Can I check your supply to see if you need more product?" And my favorite: "I am new and need to sell something to get off on the right foot." Wrong attitude with the wrong client; my company ultimately lost the account. Lesson learned the hard way: Selling works best when you do not try to sell.

Always add value to the sale. If you're assigned an account to manage, make sure your management and fulfillment role is visible to the client. That way your customer will see your influence and the value you provide.

Don't always actively sell. When you manage an account, you don't want to be perceived as a person who is only looking to generate more sales. Trying to sell too much can hurt your relationship. Always be on the lookout for opportunities, but let them come to you naturally by being "present."

CAPTAIN'S LOG
Tarpon Willie says, "Fish can pop up when you least expect it. Be prepared to steer your boat in the direction of the pod." Sales, like fishing, doesn't provide too many opportunities to land a big one, so stay attuned to your customers and be prepared. Sometimes catching the biggest fish, or clinching the biggest sale, happens when you least expect it.

Create opportunities for the client to provide value to your company. Ask your contacts to present to other customers, be a case study, provide a testimonial, or come to a show with you and hang out in your booth.

Actively pursue customer feedback. Talk with your clients about how you are doing and whether you are serving their needs. You can learn a lot from feedback. You also might be surprised at the opportunities that arise from your conversations. If the customer is reluctant to provide you with candid feedback, use a survey form or ask your sales manager to get involved.

Get to Know Your Customers

Build your client relationships every chance you get:

- Request organizational charts.
- Ask if you can go to their new-hire training.
- Offer advice in areas of which you are knowledgeable, but don't necessarily sell.
- Sponsor local events with your customer.
- Get involved in community events.

Build a "Trojan Horse" for Large Accounts

I had a colleague who used to call large account selling the "Trojan Horse" sale, referring to the incident in Homer's epic

THIS AIN'T NO FISH TALE!

One morning I was having coffee with Steve, a sales VP at a leading high-tech company. We were discussing large deals that had been closed over the last year. Steve mentioned that one of his biggest deals had actually happened by accident. On a flight to the West Coast out of Atlanta, Steve was checking e-mails on his laptop when he accidentally spilled coffee on his computer and on the leg of the passenger beside him. He quickly turned the computer over to drain the coffee from his laptop, and offered napkins to his seat companion. Steve apologized profusely as he cleaned up the mess. The man sitting next to him was very polite and quite forgiving, commenting that he'd done the same himself once or twice. The accident sparked conversation, and the other passenger revealed that he'd just been hired as COO (chief operating officer) for a large services company. Coincidentally, the company was Steve's largest customer. In fact, he'd been trying to arrange a meeting with some of the new executives within the company. As the plane traveled across the country, the two men talked business, politics, and sports. By the end of the flight, the new COO was well briefed on the business Steve had done with his company and all the other capabilities that Steve's organization could provide. As they walked off the flight, the COO handed Steve his business card and suggested a meeting. "Let's both get our key people together and see if we can do some business." That meeting resulted in a million-dollar order.

All of this over a spilled cup of coffee! You never know when you might build a relationship or enhance one that is already there. Always be prepared; some of your largest sales can happen when you least expect it.

poem, when Odysseus, seeking entrance into the city of Troy, ordered construction of a large, wooden horse. The horse's interior was left hollow so Greek warriors could hide within it. The horse was towed to Troy's city walls and presented as a gift. Thinking they had won the war, the Trojans pulled the horse inside the city and celebrated their victory. The celebration was short lived, as, in the night, the Greeks vacated the horse, swarmed the city, and established a stronghold.

You don't want to swarm your clients or conquer them; you want to serve them on an ongoing basis. Often, large accounts don't lend themselves to solo sales and account management. If an account is large or has a tremendous amount of potential, you can't meet everyone in the organization, stay involved in the organizational changes, and develop a position on a customer's issues. To establish a strong position in a client's organization and fully penetrate the account, you'll likely need help.

If it's appropriate to your business, and if the customer organization offers significant opportunities for long-term business, consider using a team of folks to work the account. If you lack the authority to build a team, you can still leverage the help of others when communicating or visiting with the customer. Remember the concept of the Trojan horse. Make your contact, establish a relationship, and then properly position others to help generate more revenue and more productivity.

Stay Involved in the Sale After the Close

For the fisherman who makes a catch, do a few fish represent a goal accomplished or just the beginning of a great run? I've learned from Tarpon Willie that rather than call it a day

CATCH SOME MORE! 171

after a few fish, successful anglers bring enough bait to put their lines back in the water to catch more fish. "You've got to know how to work your spot effectively while not overfishing or scaring off the fish," Tarpon Willie advises. It's the same in sales—always be on the lookout for other opportunities, and provide value to the buyer.

Schedule monthly meetings. Many times you inadvertently lose touch with customers. Schedule a meeting or event on a consistent basis to keep on top of their business and share news of yours.

Put your clients on a distribution list. Whether through e-mail or "snail mail," send your customers something every few weeks or months. Just be sure to personalize it in some way, so it fits their needs.

Work with your team. Check in with the implementation, fulfillment, or delivery team at least once a month. These are the folks who are delivering your product or service to your customers, and who are therefore in constant contact with those customers. They typically have great insight into the account. Know what is happening in your account and keep abreast of key issues. If you do not have a "team," work with the customer's team.

Conduct audits. Make it a practice to do an audit thirty, sixty, or ninety days after the sale. This is equivalent to a 10,000-mile checkup. Market the audit when you are making your sale, explaining that as part of the purchase process, you will visit and review how the customer is doing with your product and how effectively it has been implemented. Audits provide access to your buyer and keep you involved. Schedule that audit right after you make the sale.

Include assessments as part of your sales process. Make sure you or someone else reviews your sales process with the customer. Assessing how you worked with the client demonstrates your commitment to do a better job next time and/or to continually improve. It's the client satisfaction survey—but one that's meaningful and has teeth.

Build "Teeth" into Your Ninety-Day Audit

The following audit questions illustrate the line of inquiry an audit should take. Be sure to tailor the questions to fit your type of sale. While the general direction is appropri-

THIS AIN'T NO FISH TALE!

Early in my consulting career, I was reviewing a client's sales process, trying to determine how to make the sellers more effective and generate more revenue. Our goal was to free up more time for above-the-funnel work. Going over the numbers with the top sales directors, we saw that reps spent little time with customers once a sale was made. The client explained that by design, the reps had to transition accounts and work with new customers; after the sale, corporate staff managed the account. In a discussion with the corporate staff manager, we learned that many follow-on sales opportunities were being missed because her staff lacked the skills to identify the clients' continuing needs. She shared three e-mails from three different customers. Each clearly indicated the potential for follow-on sales. Faced with this evidence, the sales directors remarked, "Either we put those staff folks on commission, or we keep our sales reps involved a little longer." Ultimately, my client began auditing each customer ninety days after the sale to check satisfaction, identify unmet needs, and probe for further potential. With the audits in place, penetration revenue increased roughly 20 percent that first year.

ate for most sales situations, additional probing questions may be needed to diagnose a customer's issues or uncover opportunities.

 ## Catch of the Day

Leverage your preferred vendor status to fully understand your customers' needs, sell more, and develop new relationships. Customers want to align themselves with those who know their industry, or work with top companies or top personnel in the industry. They want knowledge, reliability, and a proven track record in their account manager and their vendor. Position yourself as that expert, and catch the rewards.

Always start with the "how did we do?" questions and then pursue "how else can we help?"

1. Do you feel you received a competitive solution? (Discover the client's mindset and demeanor now that the sales process has ended.)

2. Did we meet our purchasing goals? (Find out if the customer's goals and expectations for this purchase were met.)

3. Do you feel my company is meeting your needs? (Learn how well you are managing the account.)

4. Did the delivery, implementation, or service fulfillment go well? (Evaluate your postsale efforts.)

5. Are you receiving enough expertise, professionalism, and service in a timely manner? (Determine whether your skills adequately match the client's needs.)

6. Now that the sale is complete and you have had a chance to reflect, is there something you would have done differently? (Draw out flaws in the customer's process that you can help the company overcome next time around.)

7. Now that you've completed this purchase, are there other support issues or requirements you need? (Introduce the idea of additional services, offers, needs, and so on.)

8. What other areas/business units might have a need for this solution? (Determine whether other opportunities for the same offer might be present.)

9. Do you require further assistance in other areas? (Identify other opportunities and other products/services/offers within this specific area/business unit.)

10. Are there any other postsale needs that we can help facilitate? (Let the customer know you are ready and willing to help, even if there is no immediate sale to propose.)

Are You Managing Your Account Enough?

Think about a sale you made a year ago. Then answer the following questions to learn how well you are managing that account. See where you fall on the chart.

How Do You Rate as an Account Manager?

	Poor Account Manager ⟶			Great Account Manager
How often do you speak with your client?	Have not spoken since we've closed the deal	Twice a year	Once every three months	Once a month
Do you have scheduled meetings or events?	I wait until they call to schedule	I have in the past	I am going to schedule one	Yes, I have one scheduled now

	Poor Account Manager	→		Great Account Manager
Have you done an audit of the client's purchase?	No, I am leaving well enough alone	Yes, 90 days after the sale	Yes, 60 days after the sale	Yes, 30 days after the sale
Do you regularly do some work for the client?	I am off selling other stuff	I check in on status	I did when it was first sold	I help deliver and fulfill
Have you reviewed your own performance?	No review; I did a good job	An informal verbal review	A formal review by me	A formal review by my manager
Do you regularly send out notifications or hellos?	No, only when we have a new offering	My company does	Yes, every quarter	Yes, once every one to two months

Do You Have What It Takes to Catch Some More?

Many sales jobs have responsibilities to retain and grow a set of accounts. To be successful in this role requires certain competencies—the knowledge, skills, and behavior—that determine sales success. Demonstrate and master these competencies, and you enhance your ability to understand and meet customer and business needs. You'll grow professionally within your sales organization and, most important, earn more too. Refer to the table on pages 176–182.

Sample Account Management Competencies	
Competency	*Requirements*
Account Growth: Use market data and customer relationships to help systematically identify and prioritize key customer opportunities.	
Specific Sales Strategy and Tactics—Develops and executes account management sales strategy and tactics:	• Conducts pre-call planning and long-range strategy development (multiple sales-call sales cycle): 　• Develops plans to increase revenue from assigned accounts. 　• Qualifies opportunities before investing resources and time (for example, confirms budget and fit with organization). 　• Performs forecasting to determine best use of resources when planning client calls.
	• Applies selling skills: 　• Tailors selling approach to the unique needs/concerns/personalities of each customer. 　• Draws on experience and information from others to share stories and best practices with customers that help them visualize how organization can meet their needs. 　• Communicates complex concepts and applications in a simple and easy-to-understand manner. 　• Presents information effectively and persuasively and adjusts personal style accordingly. 　• Responds to customer concerns and counters objections.

Sample Account Management Competencies	
Competency	Requirements
	• Identifies opportunities for expanding usage, the sale of new products, and the sale of additional product. • Negotiates with customers, understanding total economics of the deal. • Maintains momentum in the sales process (for example, schedules the next meeting, obtains a signature). • Knows when and how to close a sale effectively, bringing in senior managers in as needed. • Displays sense of urgency and accountability in responding to and following up with accounts.
Leveraging of Resources—Uses resources to acquire knowledge and identify market opportunities:	• Uses appropriate resources to build solution, customer, and industry knowledge: • Uses internal resources to find information on customers, best practices, marketing, current white papers, and documents. • Uses external resources to build customer and industry knowledge. • Utilizes available resources to identify opportunities, track account information, and assess risk to increase efficiency of project tasks. • Understands how past customers have used your product and can apply these examples to help solve and explain current customer issues.

continued

Sample Account Management Competencies *(continued)*	
Competency	*Requirements*
Relationship Management—Builds and maintains relationships to deepen advocacy and build influence:	• Deepens relationships with key customers, understanding their personality types and personal interests, and uses this knowledge to enhance influence with customers; introduces customers to others within organization in order to deepen customers' ties.
	• Engages with clients at all levels of the clients' organization.
	• Speaks to a variety of customers from different departments, at different levels, and in large or small groups.
	• Serves as a trusted adviser to clients (is requested at meetings; executive-level clients respond quickly to e-mails/phone calls; clients ask for advice).
	• Makes self available on-site as needed in order to facilitate communication with clients and ensure that customer needs are being met.
	• Knows customer problems and anticipates their needs.
	• Seeks and maintains high levels of customer satisfaction: • Resolves customer issues. • Sets up quarterly reviews with clients to ensure organization is aligned with key client initiatives. • Maintains client relationships even if a particular opportunity is lost.

Sample Account Management Competencies	
Competency	*Requirements*
Customer Focus: Demonstrates a strong understanding of the fundamentals of the customer's business and applies this knowledge to diagnose business issues, facilitate decision-making, resolve key issues, gain approvals, and implement solutions.	
Business Acumen—Understands, articulates, and applies the key drivers (such as markets, competitors, customers) and metrics of the client's business and industry:	• Demonstrates a command of the customer strategy, key measures, industry, competitive environment and implications of issues: • Reviews summaries from support staff on relevant industry trends, issues, best practices, competitive environment, and implications affecting the customer's business and/or industry.

	• Uses knowledge of the customer's business to assess findings and shape solutions:
	  • Probes for business challenges in order to assess opportunities.
	  • Develops dialogue with customers on business issues and trends.
	  • Addresses customer business problems when positioning solutions.
	  • Supplies customers with counsel that meets specific business needs and demonstrates ROI.
	  • Continually updates value proposition to ensure relevance to customer needs.
	  • Develops business response to RFPs and RFIs.
	  • Understands corporate finance fundamentals, financial (numerical) impact on the client's business, and how to prepare and present the ROI.

continued

Sample Account Management Competencies *(continued)*	
Competency	*Requirements*
Organizational Acumen—Understands the social dynamics and the operational and decision-making processes within client organizations and applies this knowledge to shape, advocate, and position solutions:	• Understands organizational processes and how different customer structures affect decision-making quality and speed: • Knows the key stakeholders and influencers (at director level and above) in the account, and develops and cultivates a network of supporters. • Asks questions to identify broader needs of key stakeholders and decision-makers. • Identifies and cultivates relationships with coaches at target companies to gain entry to new relationships.
	• Influences the opinions and decisions of clients using understanding of client's organizational processes: • Assesses the organizational, strategic, and process implications of the client organization to develop appropriate and practical recommendations or solutions. • Understands and uses the current politics in the organization to get the right things done (for example, talks to executives about their concerns). • Understands how budgets are built, consumed, and frozen.

Sample Account Management Competencies	
Competency	*Requirements*
Teamwork: Works collaboratively with others to identify, prioritize, and maximize customer opportunities and long-term organizational success.	

Team Creation—Builds team with appropriate skill set to serve clients successfully:	• Uses internal network to discover individuals' skill sets.
	
	• Organizes teams for sales opportunities:
	  • Navigates internal processes to recruit and retain people with the right talent.
	  • Stays aware of when team might need to be restructured based on changing business need.

Sales Approach—Works with team to determine selling approach and ensure effective account calls:	• Understands the working styles and needs of individuals and uses this knowledge to ensure effective and timely delivery of deliverables (for example, responses to RFPs and RFIs, contract completion):
	  • Involves senior managers in proposal reviews as needed.
	  • Oversees timelines and process logistics.
	  • Updates senior managers on account progress and key initiatives.
	  • Describes and positions offers or solutions, bringing in others for deep product expertise and positioning.
	
	• Differentiates value proposition versus the competition:
	  • Identifies opportunities for expanding usage and obtains customer support.
	  • Works to frame and respond to potential cross-selling.
	  • Sets expectations for sales meetings.
	  • Oversees delivery, both informally and formally, to monitor customer satisfaction and contract progress.

continued

Sample Account Management Competencies *(continued)*	
Competency	*Requirements*
Problem Solving—Contributes to team problem solving:	• Prioritizes account leads and responsibilities and discusses tradeoffs with team members when appropriate.
	• Surfaces and responds to objections to products and/or suggested approaches.
	• Maintains regular communication with team members (for example, via voice mails, e-mails) so everyone understands what the others are working on.
	• Gathers information (from internal tools/ resources, independent research, key contacts, own observations, or data collected from the customer) to accurately define a problem or an issue.
	• Proactively collaborates with teammates to anticipate and respond to issues that could impact sales (for instance, the customer's business, points in the sales cycle, and change in scope)

THIS AIN'T NO FISH TALE!

Living in Florida, I get to experience the "thrill" of hurricanes and the feelings of unease and vulnerability that the thought of a big storm can bring. One weekend, I was wandering around a home superstore when an employee approached from behind a kiosk. "Are you aware of the latest weather patterns regarding hurricanes?" he inquired. "I'm working with [this store] to help our customers understand what the threats are and how homeowners can protect against them." Having a little bit of time, and not a small amount of curiosity, I took the bait, indicating interest. At that, the employee shared some alarming statistics: the growing number of named storms each year, the expanding diameter of the hurricanes' eye, the increasing wind speeds, and last, the escalating amount of damage a typical storm victim suffers. "The good news," he assured me, "is that you can take simple measures to help protect your home: new windows, storm shutters, clearing tree limbs from around the house, drainage systems, power generator . . ." He had me. With hurricane season fast approaching, I thought about how my home would be affected and how unprepared I was. That very day, I expanded my shopping list and purchased some products that offered hurricane protection.

This tale illustrates a salesman who was not selling, but informing—making me aware. He had a great elevator pitch and worked my emotions. He made sure I knew the trends, issues, and practices around hurricanes and hurricane protection. He helped identify my need, exposed a deficiency, created urgency, and stimulated a sale. It was a great example of solid account—and customer—management!

CHAPTER NINE

Know When to Throw Some Back or Cut the Line

IS THE SALE WORTH YOUR TIME AND EFFORT?

I remember a time, ten years back, when Tarpon Willie and I were fishing for tarpon under a bridge in Sarasota. It was early morning, just before dawn. We saw tarpon rolling and striking bait, congregating just off the bridge pilings. We anchored up on one side of the bridge to allow our lines to flow with the tides. All signs appeared to be in our favor: the tides, the calm morning, the bait, and the day's temperature. We threw out our lines and were rewarded with a quick hit. But just as quickly, the fish fought back, yanking the line across the barnacles of the bridge and swimming to freedom. To avoid the bridge and its many dangers, we let the anchor line out a little and threw out four more fishing poles. Within ten minutes, we had a "hat trick" (three tarpon on three lines). Tarpon Willie grabbed one pole; I grabbed another. The third, we pumped hard to hook the fish. Then we set the rod back in its holder, ready to pull it in once we landed the first two. Focused on reeling in the tarpon, while avoiding the bridge and the

CAPTAIN'S LOG

"If you only have one shot, is that the fish you want to catch?"
—Tarpon Willie

rush of oncoming boat traffic, Tarpon Willie yelled, "Why not cut that third tarpon. There's a heck of a lot of competition for our attention. Why hold out for the trifecta when the exacta's a sure thing?" Ever the optimist, I was reluctant to let the third fish go. "We have 'em all hooked," I argued. "All we have to do is reel them in!" Knowing that catching tarpon was a big deal for me, Tarpon Willie chuckled, shook his head, and said, "Have at 'em!"

CAPTAIN'S LOG

Tarpon Willie says, "Don't wait for the perfect fish; you'll never catch it!" As a sales rep, your goal is to use your time wisely, always focusing on making better, more profitable sales. Although this chapter provides advice on when to throw back a sale or cut one loose, I'm talking about those extreme deals that can hurt your efficiency or profitability, or go beyond the scope of your company's ability to deliver. I would never advocate passing up good deals on the line in favor of a "better" deal that hasn't yet surfaced—and maybe never will.

As we continued the fight, Willie kept shouting advice: "Hit the fish!" "Give him some slack!" "Move to the front of the boat!" "Keep your line from crossing mine!" Things were happening so fast, it was hard to keep up. As the fight continued, my fish would not cooperate. He kept heading toward the bridge—a sure danger given the pilings and jagged rocks beneath the surface. As I tried to pull the tarpon back, my line crossed Willie's. Within an instant, both fish were gone. The friction had snapped the lines. My disappointment was palpable. Those fish had double-punched us!

Fortunately, we still had that third fish on the line. I congratulated myself on making the right call. Just as I picked the pole out of its holder, I felt a quick tug and then the fish went limp. I kept reeling. As the fish came closer to the surface, it was making short runs and fighting oddly. Then, I saw the tail—wriggling in the mouth of a six-foot hammerhead. I'd hooked the fish, but when I left it hanging, a predator moved in for the kill. All three fish were gone. Tarpon Willie spoke not a word, but his glance said it all. Whether fishing or selling, sometimes you have to let some go in order to preserve what you have!

How do fishermen decide which fish to throw back, or when to cut the line? In a tournament that judges both the number of fish caught and the collective weight of the catch, the answer is not always obvious, yet it needs to be made quickly so the fish can either be boated or returned to the sea unharmed. As the day progresses, the desire to keep those smaller fish may turn to regret when a bigger guy swims by. However, the flip side of that argument can also cause grief. How do you know another larger fish is going to come along? If it doesn't, and you miss the opportunity, can you recoup?

Sales reps often face the same dilemma. How many times have you pondered whether a sale is really worthwhile? You may wonder whether so much time and energy devoted to one customer is causing you to miss other opportunities. It may be the wrong deal, a tough customer, or a poor strategic match. Yet once you've devoted time to a sale, it can be tough to turn the boat around and pull in the lines. All reps need to heed the warning signs that it's time to cut their losses and move on to friendlier waters.

Beware High-Maintenance Deals

Predator fish—mackerel, shark, tuna, jack—are fun to catch, but also require enormous effort. They can hook a line and run with it, from one end of the boat to the other, out to sea and back, over and under the anchor line. Fishermen must be prepared for the challenges, or they may find those big fish too much to handle.

Similarly, high-maintenance deals demand significant resources, starting with a committed sales team that's able to devote the required time and level of responsiveness.

THIS AIN'T NO FISH TALE!

I learned this lesson well when I caught an opportunity with a decent-sized company shortly after moving into consulting. Ultimately, it turned out to be the wrong division for a major sale, but hindsight is a great teacher, and I hadn't learned the lesson yet. I spent lots of time with the client, answered all the questions, and sold a small project, which consequently ate up huge chunks of my time. Later, when a "sure thing" opportunity with another customer surfaced, I couldn't get away for an in-person meeting. In my place, I sent another junior consultant. My participation in the meeting thus was limited to a conference call. During the meeting, I could tell things weren't going well, but being 500 miles away, there wasn't much I could do. I had told myself this opportunity was like a fish in the cooler, ready to be taken ashore.

I was wrong. I never got the assignment. The client later told me that the company signed on with my competitor because she showed up with her full team. While the company initially saw me as the right consultant, it interpreted my inability to visit the office as stemming from either a lack of interest or lack of time. In the end, the hours I devoted to that first, small sale lost me a big one—$15,000 versus $125,000. I never made that mistake again.

I'm not advocating that just because a deal is difficult or a customer demands a lot of time, you cut the line or throw them back. That would be a simple solution, and lazy or undisciplined to boot! Turn your back on a hard sale, and you run the risk of becoming a soft seller who, in pursuit of the "right" deal, allows several good ones to get away.

Seek out the sales that best align with your abilities, your product or service, or your strategic direction. Reps who want to sell anything and everything risk overcommitting themselves or promising beyond their ability to fulfill the sale. Don't let the lure of reaching quota or making a quick dollar overshadow reason. You can lose your reputation and your credibility. Think long-term. If you're not sure about your or your company's ability to handle a sale, seek your manager's input.

Know When to Throw Some Back

There are many fish in the sea. The following signals tell you it's time to end your struggle and look elsewhere.

Too much time with one client at the expense of another. This is a classic sign that you may be out of sync or rhythm with your catch. This time spent—or lost—will manifest itself through lost productivity or the loss of other sales or customers. A customer that demands too much time, when your sales process or methodology does not allow it, can make you ineffective with your other responsibilities. If you expect to stay competitive in your business, don't allow a customer to trap you. Maintain some distance or remove yourself from the opportunity or account. In the worst-case scenario, cut your ties altogether and move on to another opportunity.

As Tarpon Willie says, "When you're fishing, always give yourself time to check out your favorite spots on the way back to the dock, especially if the tides are right. Don't squander all your time in one spot and miss the feeding frenzy that might be happening just below the dock." Spend too much time with one client, and you could miss opportunities to expand your client base and acquire new sales.

 **Catch of the Day**

Unless you want to withdraw completely from an account, don't become too uninvolved. If you lose touch with your account, you lose touch with that customer's issues. If you plan to sell more in this account eventually, or provide thought leadership to your customer, keep a finger on the pulse.

Too many other customer commitments. If you have too many lines in the water and hook multiple fish, you won't be able to catch them all. Worse, you might lose them all. On the surface, this seems like a great problem to have, but it can threaten your reputation and quality. Tarpon Willie would say, "They're biting at the naked hook." Here's the problem with overabundance: If you can't support all the fish on the line, then you risk losing not just one, but the whole catch because you're stretched too thin. The solution is to assess the potential of each account and then either get help, or cut the line.

Wrong financials. Are your financial goals, company goals, or your larger quota commitments going to be met if you accept this work? Make sure you understand the ramifications of the deal before you pursue it. Be wary of these thoughts:

- "I can make it up on the next sale."
- "He will buy more the next time."

- "This is to get the foot in the door."
- "Selling to a client of this size and with this reputation will win me more business."
- "It's a strategic account."

Lack of personnel. Before you chase a deal, sell a deal, commit to a deal, or chase certain aspects of a deal, make sure you have the right personnel to fulfill the requirements. Don't overlook this point or assume that you can make it work with the "wrong" people.

 Tackle Box

WAYS TO DISENTANGLE YOURSELF FROM AN ACCOUNT

- **Introduce others.** The more people you can involve to leverage your time, the more you can accomplish all together, and the less the client will rely solely upon you.

- **Make the sales process clear.** Explain the sales process, the handoffs, and the transitions your organization will move through to best serve the client's needs. Position the handoffs as being in the client's best interest.

- **Set expectations.** Establish what commitments you can or cannot make. Discuss expectations during the sales process so your customer won't view any disengagement on your part as a "bait and switch" ploy.

- **Tactfully make yourself unavailable.** If an account is demanding too much of your time, fully transition the account to someone else. Don't cut and run; make sure the customer has the right support. Then respectfully let the new contact handle the customer since you "are not available."

Aggressive timing. When customers buy something, they usually want it "yesterday." Make sure you establish your timelines early and understand the commitments you are making. If the timelines and commitments present too much of a stretch, tactfully push back prior to the sale to create some slack in the line. Pursue these avenues to try to push back:

1. Explain the cost ramifications of moving quickly (for example, an expediting charge for faster service). If fast turnaround is an imperative, the customer may be willing to pay for it.

2. Make it clear that your best people will not be available until after the requested date.

3. Clarify your fulfillment process and explain the quality conflicts, or other ramifications that may be incurred by rushing the process.

If the customer adamantly refuses to budge the timeline and your team will be stretched, don't take the deal. Chances are, your competitors will have the same issues.

Needs do not match. Do not make deals that will not match your customers' needs, wants, or desires. You will disappoint them, and they will blame you for selling them something they did not need.

Let Your Sales Funnel Be Your Guide

To determine whether a deal is worth the time, review your current sales pipeline and the number of deals you have in the funnel. Estimate the average time spent in each step for each deal and the total time required per deal. Apply these results to the deals you are working on. This will help you understand the total time it will take to move the current deals through the pipeline. Now look at the individual deals. If a deal is taking longer for a certain step or for the complete process, decide whether the outcome of the deal will be worth the effort or the time invested.

For example, the following Funnel Analysis of Average Deals shows that "Alex," the sales rep, spends an average of sixteen hours on each deal. Each deal, on average, has a value of $5,000. Alex spends seven hours—almost half the total time devoted to the deal—in the first two stages, identifying and qualifying the sale. The proposal stage takes another five hours. Alex devotes so much time to the critical up-front work, it takes only one hour to close the sale.

THIS AIN'T NO FISH TALE!

One of my former partners had a client that used to ask for extreme deadlines. If a project would take ten weeks, the client pressured for completing it in five. My partner would push back, but so would the client, replying, "I'll give you two of my best people to help you meet the deadline." After being burned a few times by the assistance of these "helpers" and getting bogged down in training, coaching, or fulfilling their needs, my partner came up with a foolproof response. Next time a client asked for a cost savings or rush job and offered help to get it done, my partner responded, "Our price and timing to meet your objectives is $50,000 with a ten-week timeline. If you want your personnel to help out, it'll cost $60,000 and take twelve weeks." Clearly he was joking, but he got the point across: Don't sacrifice quality!

Funnel Analysis of Average Deals—
Average Time and Value Per Deal:

Sales Process Step	Time Per Step
Identify	5 hours
Qualify	2 hours
Propose	5 hours
Close	1 hour
Fulfill	3 hours
Total	16 hours
Average Deal Value	$5,000

In the following Funnel Analysis of Current Deal, Alex is facing a deal that was relatively easy to identify and qualify but is getting bogged down in the proposal stage. Alex estimates eight hours for the proposal stage because of the lengthy RFP (request for proposal) that must be completed, and the customer's penchant for multiple meetings to review the offer with successive management levels. On the back end of the deal, Alex expects fulfillment to eat up another ten hours because of the customization required and subsequent handholding needed to guide the customer through to delivery. This current deal is estimated to be twice the work—thirty-two hours versus sixteen—yet it will generate only $1,000 more in revenue. Is it worth it?

Funnel Analysis of Current Deal—
Estimated Time and Value of Current Deal

Sales Process Step	Time Per Step
Identify	3 hours
Qualify	1 hour
Propose	8 hours
Close	10 hours
Fulfill	10 hours
Total	32 hours
Average Deal Value	$6,000

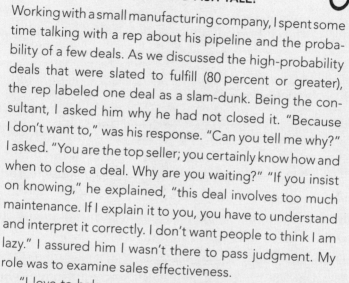

THIS AIN'T NO FISH TALE!

Working with a small manufacturing company, I spent some time talking with a rep about his pipeline and the probability of a few deals. As we discussed the high-probability deals that were slated to fulfill (80 percent or greater), the rep labeled one deal as a slam-dunk. Being the consultant, I asked him why he had not closed it. "Because I don't want to," was his response. "Can you tell me why?" I asked. "You are the top seller; you certainly know how and when to close a deal. Why are you waiting?" "If you insist on knowing," he explained, "this deal involves too much maintenance. If I explain it to you, you have to understand and interpret it correctly. I don't want people to think I am lazy." I assured him I wasn't there to pass judgment. My role was to examine sales effectiveness.

"I love to help my customers," the rep proclaimed. "I love to add value; and I certainly love to sell our products. I believe in what I do. Yet some cases I need to pass up. It's demanding, but not in a good way. The customer takes forever to make up its mind. When we close a deal, the customer treats me, our support staff, and our delivery team like incompetents. We have bent over backwards for the company, and have cut or reduced our prices while adding more people to the account. The time we've devoted to this client has hindered our ability to serve others, killed our profits, and crushed the team's morale. As I look at my funnel, I have more deals with less probability, but a greater chance of profitability. This client buys from us because no one else will serve it. It is still in my funnel because we are trying to figure out how we can make it a win/win. If we can make the company understand how we can best serve it, then we will. If not, we are going to pass."

If you have time to pursue a sale because your funnel is light, then keep on it even if that deal is taking a long time, or is high-maintenance. However, if the deal is not profitable, cut your line and fish elsewhere.

Strive for Win/Win Deals

A key component to a successful deal is the joint feeling that each party has won in the negotiations and in the purchase or sale. To be truly effective, always strive for this win/win deal. It's not about winning at the other's expense, but negotiating a deal, in which the terms and conditions match both parties' expectations and requirements.

A sale that leaves one party feeling that it gave up too much is an unsuccessful deal. If, as a seller, you command too high of a price, too long of a time frame, or too many concessions,

Tackle Box

TO FISH OR NOT TO FISH?

This simple test can help you decide whether you should keep a deal on the line:

- **F**—Financials Fit? Do the financials meet our strategic goals and objectives?
- **I**—Implement it? Can we implement and fulfill it within the right parameters?
- **S**—Support it? Can we support it with the right product and people?
- **H**—Handle it? Do the timing and customer's needs match ours?

your client will not return. Even worse, the client will broadcast its belief that you took advantage of the company. The client may be all smiles to you, since the company does not want to lose face and admit you beat it in negotiations, but deep down, it feels cheated.

On the other hand, if you give away your boat and tackle to win a deal, you and your organization will be stuck with the consequences. These can range from an urge to "stick it to" someone, a feeling of regret about your failed sales process, the need to fight off other customers who want the same great terms, or the cheapening of your offer in the market. In any case, as a seller, you lose. Your customer will move on, but you have to live with your decisions for a long time. If it's not a win/win, don't sell it.

A Lesson Learned

During the early days of my corporate career, I had a sales channel management job that entailed identifying, qualifying, selecting, and negotiating relationships with telemarketing vendors to sell small business services to our customer base. I offered contracts to multimillion-dollar telemarketing companies. As you can imagine, I was a popular target for many large firms. Sales reps figured if they could land my employer, they'd have a great name to use as a reference, on top of a potentially very large contract.

My company's size and brand name gave me a clear advantage, and I would try to extract everything I could from the vendors who approached me. At the time, I saw this strategy as a win/win: I got a great deal on pricing while the vendor got a long-term contract with a prestige client. In most cases, I took pride in the terms I negotiated, and within my company, I was seen as a good vendor and contract manager. My perception began to change one afternoon, however, when I learned that one of my vendors was not renewing his contract with my company. The conversation went something like this: "We love doing business with you and your team," the vendor explained, and then added, "but along with the big-company status come problems. We've tried to make this work, but we're losing money. Your terms, conditions, and price are killing us. We hoped we could make the first contract work; now we know we can't. Your product is complex and requires more skilled telemarketing reps to sell your services. Yet your terms squeeze us so much that we can't train, develop, and retain the talent we need. We don't want to run the risk of jeopardizing our name and reputation and potentially damaging your customer relationships. So we're passing on your business. We really enjoyed working with you, but we can't any longer." He went on to say, "We know your contract is nonnegotiable and that many vendors will jump at this opportunity, so we won't ask for concessions that you most likely can't live with. We wish you the best of luck."

I was speechless; I never had been confronted with a situation like this. I was losing a vendor that had been a good team player. I started to question myself: Had I demanded too much? Was this vendor speaking the truth? Most important, in looking at the numbers, it was my most productive vendor. What was I going to do? I would miss my objective if the vendor left, and I had no one teed up to take over. And if he was right, could I even attract another vendor in time to sell this product under these terms? Thinking the situation through, I still could not believe I was being "cut loose." Yet, now I understand the reason, and grudgingly, I saw his point. I'd been beating up my vendors to get the best deal possible for my company; I never considered their side. A few days later, I called the vendor. I asked him what terms were required for him to stay on my account. I expect he almost fell out of his chair. After a couple of offers and some minor details, we agreed on new terms that represented a win/win for both of us.

 Catch of the Day

Never make someone feel beaten down and/or uncomfortable with the terms of a deal; you might not have a chance to make another one with that customer.

Even when you hold position of strength, strive for deals that work for both parties. A true partnership considers both sides. Discuss your concerns, issues, and thoughts. Then negotiate or agree to deals that work for all.

CHAPTER TEN

Follow the Fisherman's Code

TREAT PEOPLE WELL AND ALWAYS
BE READY TO EXTEND A HAND

Another early morning on the water with Tarpon Willie: We had caught our bait and perfectly timed the tides. It promised to be a heck of a morning. If we rushed just a little, we would catch the "bull tide," the peak high tide that often follows a full moon. Just around the point, we came upon a small boat stationary in the channel. We assumed its occupant was fishing for bait. But as we got

CAPTAIN'S LOG

"Load your boat with people who can help you find the fish. Always be generous—there's enough fish for everyone."—Tarpon Willie

closer and slowed our motor, we came upon a stranded crabber tinkering with an engine that wouldn't start. Seeing us approach, the crabber waved and called out to flag our attention. Tarpon Willie eyed our brimming bucket of succulent bait, our poles at the ready, and the perfect tides. "I guess our decision is made," he said. "Let's help this fella out. The fish can wait. We might miss the fish this morning, but we won't miss the chance to help."

On the water, there is an unwritten rule that if you see a boat in distress, you stop to help. At any sign of trouble, a pro slows to ensure a fellow boater's motor is functioning, helps him off a sand bar, or tows him to shore if needed. Leaving someone stranded is downright unacceptable—no ifs, ands, or buts.

The same holds true in sales: Never leave a team member marooned; always be ready to extend a helping hand. A top sales rep who is truly a winner willingly shares insights and expertise; not in a boastful way—no one learns from a bragging egoist—but with the aim to help others expand their repertoire of skills and know-how. It creates success for the team and the company.

Mark Your Spot and Share Your Knowledge

The expression "X marks the spot" applies to both fishing and selling. When they've found a profitable fishing hole or

THIS AIN'T NO FISH TALE!

I remember consulting with a highly autonomous sales organization. This organization was a loose confederation of pirates—each salesperson acted like a minifranchise. The reps were competitive with each other, rarely checked in, and didn't enter necessary information into their Sales Force Automation tool. Reps routinely sandbagged their performance numbers to look good at the quarter's end and outperform the other reps. Bottom line: the organization focused more on itself than on the competition or the customer. This company's sales results couldn't compare with other companies that built more cohesive sales organizations—ones in which the reps focus outward, not inward.

landed a big customer, winners know to mark their territory, learn from their success, and help others by sharing their wealth.

World-class, professional fishermen refer to tide charts, journals, and records of their catches, and logs of their coordinates so they can return to that spot again and again. They document the bait, lures, and even the tackle they used to get the big fish so they can follow that formula on yet another day. They do not brag about their catch, yet may subtly, and without vanity, respond to a question: "Catchin' anything today?" or "How'd ya do?"

Salespeople should do the same. Whether it's a success journal, a deal review or funnel meeting, or a postmortem deal analysis, salespeople can learn from every situation. Successful reps evaluate results, seek guidance from others, and keep a log of the factors and conditions that helped them identify the opportunity and close the sale. They share experiences and lessons to leverage talent, and teach and develop others.

CAPTAIN'S LOG

Tarpon Willie says, "Know how you caught your fish; know how you lost it. If you review, you remember. If you listen, you learn." In other words, know what you did, how you did it, and when you did it. Put them together, and you understand what it takes to be a great fisherman and a great salesperson.

Review Deals as a Team

Listen in on the radio chatter among professional anglers and you'll hear them comparing notes about their day's catch, explaining how and where they caught the fish. Usually, the pros communicate on some high or low channel that only their peers and friends know about. They are sharing information and helping each other.

Sales organizations benefit from similar conversations, referred to as funnel reviews or pipeline meetings. These meetings allow reps to review, scrutinize, and analyze all the nuances of the sale and each step in the sales process. If approached correctly, these meetings allow all team members to share experiences and learn from one another.

The purpose of a funnel or deal review meeting is *not* to brag, but to explain the details or accomplishments to others and seek feedback or help if needed. Think of the meeting as a dress rehearsal, with the chance for "free" advice from peers or superiors prior to getting in front of a client.

Typically, the sales manager or region manager and his or her direct reports attend the deal meeting. Depending on the size of an organization, other divisions or other sales groups may participate, too. These meetings usually occur weekly or bimonthly and last no more than an hour or two. (Frequency may vary depending on the length of an organization's sales cycle and whether deals are transactional or more long-term.) The more experienced the reps or managers are, the more quality advice will be free flowing.

Catch of the Day

Your colleagues will tell you if your "bait" or "chum" smells, whereas your customers may be reluctant to hurt your feelings and just avoid you. Whenever you can, try to gain experience and perspective from others.

Deal meetings may intimidate neophyte sellers, and frankly, may bore those more experienced. Yet if managed correctly, they can provide valuable insight and perspective on key deals you may have in your net. The right insights might even tip you off to things you would have overlooked or not expected. In many cases, the feedback you receive from your peers and subordinates can be tougher than that you receive from your clients or prospects. Such unvarnished truths can help. Moreover, don't shy away from questioning others on their deals. You always want to try to help others catch their fish! "Toughen your skin" and prepare yourself for fielding a similar question or observation from a client.

What to Discuss and Review

An effective sales review meeting or log focuses on the following types of information. (See the Deal Review Meeting Template on pages 210–211 for an example of how you can prepare for the meeting and present the details of your deal.)

Customer details

Identify the how, what, when, and where of a sale. For example:

- **How** you uncovered your customer. Potentially, this information will help uncover other opportunities.
- **What** the customer's industry and products are, and also, what makes the account interesting or challenging. This discussion may prod others to draw comparisons to other opportunities.
- **When** the discovery was made. In other words, what was the dynamic that caused you or your customer to seek each other out—budgeting season, merger activities, change in management?
- **Where** the customer is located—region, district, city, and so on. Location may spur discussion about who might be available to help you, as well as other clients in the same area that might be references, or prospects with similar needs.

Issues customers are facing

Clearly articulate the issues a potential customer is facing to give your team a good understanding of what your platform or pitch is all about. Your team members may have clients grappling with similar issues. Their feedback can help you to craft your solution.

Proposed solutions

Explain the offer or solution that you are proposing. Provide sufficient details, including why you propose your approach.

Key differences

Identify how your solution or approach is different—what distinguishes it from the competition? Thinking this through helps you contrast your offer from competitors' and highlight your competitive advantage.

Contractual terms

Test your assumptions around cost, delivery dates, terms and conditions, and so on. Terms are critical to discuss at any deal review meeting. Formulating good answers to tough questions from peers and superiors will prepare you for customer queries and thicken your skin.

Negotiation points

Explain your bargaining advantage or negotiation position and approach. This is your "fishing-poker" strategy. It may include a backup plan, if someone is in your spot or on your tail and trying to jump ahead. You may need a fallback plan or a concession or two if it helps you close a deal. Testing your plan with your peers puts you in a better position when you're negotiating with the customer.

Proposed close dates

Explain how long it will take to move your deal through the funnel. Include time required to get to the next stage: when you will have a face-to-face, when you will propose a solution, when you anticipate closing the deal, and when you will deliver. Discussion of close dates helps assure proper financial forecasting and alerts the organization of the need to gear up for implementation or fulfillment of your sale.

Help wanted

Make your needs known if you would benefit from help. Ask for help up-front. Don't wait until a deal is closed or close to it. If you aren't sure of your needs, ask for the group opinion, or put them on notice that you might need help. Try to get the specific names and/or commitments from individuals. Don't get caught trying to finish a deal and find out too late that your support is enjoying a day at the beach, while you're on the water.

Risks

Potential risks lurk in every deal. Profile potential threats with your group to gain insights or guidance. Be prepared to consider and discuss the following:

- **Competitive Risks.** What are all of your suspected competitive threats, and how do you plan to defend against them? Be prepared with at least three strong answers. For example, "This customer has bought from XYZ competitor in the past and wants a bid from them again on this deal. To help convince or persuade the customer to select us, I will: (1) Explain that we work with many of your peers and understand your industry; (2) Use customer testimonials and examples of customers who have chosen our offering over the competitors; and (3) Make sure our terms and conditions meet their requirements and put pressure on the competitor's proposal."

- **Risks Within the Client Organization.** What challenges do you face from your customer? Remember the BAIT acronym—and make sure you understand the risks around budgeting, authority, other "interested" parties, and timing. Risks also may include organizational changes within your client's company, or the reshuffling of executives. Probe your client for these issues and discuss them with your peers and superiors.

- **Other External Risks.** What other risks might you uncover as you move through the funnel? Seasonal factors could affect the selling cycle, as could a merger or acquisition. Environmental issues may arise. Understanding and or discussing these risks will help you plan for contingencies.

- **Risks Within Your Organization.** This arguably might be the most important risk to your deal, and quite possibly future deals. You do not want to pursue a sale or make the sale if your organization cannot support, fulfill, or implement the solution, due to the nature of the sale or other competing deals or agendas. Make sure all your internal needs are available to make this transaction a success during and after the sales process. By clearly identifying any internal weak spots, you will challenge your "crew" to get ready and be prepared for the "fishing trip" ahead.

Other opportunities

Any good salesperson will always be on the lookout for other deals that might be possible with this prospect. Even early in a deal, always be thinking of ways to help address your client's other needs. Considering these early on will keep you focused on doing a great job and proving to the client you are worthy of more business.

As with any human interaction, there are no "definites." The key ingredient in coaching is to take an interest in helping others. You're not accountable for your colleagues' performance, but you can aid in their development, and learn some new things in the process.

CAPTAIN'S LOG

Tarpon Willie says, "Allow yourself to be taught. Even the most proficient learn from good advice." *Athletes, corporate executives, and most professionals continually engage in training, learning and keeping their skills current. You should, too.*

Tackle Box

NAVIGATING A DEAL REVIEW MEETING

A deal review meeting presents the opportunity to discuss your deal and seek guidance. It also allows you to provide input or offer advice to others who might need your help. Before or after you present your information, pay attention and offer opinions regarding the process or results of your colleagues.

- Don't criticize, but do question and probe as appropriate in order to help a rep.

- Share your experiences in similar situations, or share approaches that have worked for you.

- Unless you're a sales manager, don't try to manage another rep's process; instead, quiz or provide feedback based upon your experiences and successes.

A Deal Review Meeting Template

Parent Company

_____

Key Subsidiaries or Divisions

_____

Annual Revenue

_____

Number of Employees

_____

Location

_____

Opportunity Description (How, What, When, Where)

_____

Client Issues

_____

Proposed Solution

_____

How Will Our Solution Help Client? How Are We Different?

_____

Contractual Terms

_____

Negotiation Points

_____

Contact Name/Title/Phone/E-mail
_____

Role and Influence in Organization
_____

Relationship with Our Company
_____

Stage in Funnel
_____

Next Steps
_____

Tools Needed or Used
_____

Participants or Help Needed
_____

Expected Outcome
_____

Timing to Move to Next Step and to Close
_____

Potential Risks to Deal
_____

Other Opportunities
_____

Publicize, but Don't Brag

On the water or on the dock, seasoned pros prefer not to publicize their catch too loudly. Once they do, their fishing spots become tourist attractions and as soon as they start their boats, other boats follow. There's a fine line between publicizing and bragging.

Same with sales: brag too much about success with a certain account and you may well rub your coworkers the wrong way. Worse yet, just as blood in the water attracts sharks, success brings on the competition. Become a braggart, and competitors hearing about your victory may try to swoop in and try to penetrate or "unsell" your account.

The trick is to know when to discuss your success and how to do it in a way that does not turn colleagues off or competitors on. The following tips can help you promote, without being perceived as a self-promoter.

Know your point. Before opening your mouth, understand your purpose for publicizing your sale. Do you want the attention in order to position yourself for more sales, or are you tooting your own horn just to broadcast your success and pat yourself on the back? If it's the former, then your intentions are in the right place. If it's the latter, you're not doing yourself any favors. Your "me so great" message may be read as arrogance. Granted, it's a fine line, but if you're a good salesperson, and understand your goal of selling more product, then you'll typically be more selective and deliberate with your message. When you've thought about your goal and what you want to accomplish by announcing your sale, make your message short and sweet. If your team wants more details, let them pull the information out of you.

Be confident, yet humble. The point of broadcasting your success is to communicate that you succeeded. Be proud of this fact. At the same time, also acknowledge the support of others, whether those on the team, a helpful client, or wisdom gained though trial and experience that helped you succeed in this deal.

Know your audience. Ask yourself whether these are the people with whom you should be discussing your sale. Why do

THIS AIN'T NO FISH TALE!

I attended an end-of-period sales meeting where a sales manager was handing out awards to the top sellers. The gifts were gift cards to a local restaurant. The first two winners were very excited to receive their awards and accepted the praise of their manager and colleagues. The third winner, John, accepted his award quietly, thanked the crowd, and sat back down. When the manager asked him to say a few words, he declined, saying it was his job to sell and he'd done nothing special. Hearing this, I figured John was humble and didn't want the attention. Walking out of the meeting, I overheard one of the reps say to another, "Can you believe John? He is so arrogant; he acts as if he doesn't work hard and is only doing what's asked of him. He's making us all look bad in comparison." I mentioned this comment to the sales manager. "I've heard this before," the manager replied. "John is not arrogant; he really does not like the attention. I've told him he should take more credit for working hard and doing a great job. He's been our top seller for years. He just won't do it. He downplays it so much that it bothers the other reps and they resent him for it." The moral of the story: Take praise gracefully, but take it. Downplay your achievements, and people may think you're sandbagging.

they need to know? What will they do with the information? How will it help you or them? Make sure your message will be received positively, or keep it to yourself.

Tell only the truth. Only discuss deals that are closed, or signed, sealed, and delivered. Do not discuss deals that would, should, or could happen. Discussing a deal that has not closed except within your own internal sales meetings is not good practice. You could jinx a deal by bragging about it and come off looking like a braggadocio, not to mention silly, if the deal ultimately falls through. As Tarpon Willie would say, "A fish ain't caught 'til it's caught."

CAPTAIN'S LOG

Tarpon Willie says, "Don't just show people your spot; teach them how to catch fish." Try to help others a little every week, and you will provide and receive great benefits.

Make sure the sale is current. Old deals are yesterday's news. In sales, your success is determined by "what have you done for me lately?" If your sale is more than thirty days old, keep your mouth shut until you win a new one. Chances are that most people have heard about it. Once you've mentioned a sale to someone, don't bring it up again unless they ask.

Learn to take compliments. When you receive praise or are recognized for an achievement, a sale, or a job well done, never downplay the praise or make a comment that discredits it, such as, "Not a big deal." Having others talk about your success is exactly what you want to happen. Enjoy the attention.

Discuss your accomplishments in person. Try to avoid detailing achievements via e-mail, mail, or phone. Written communication about a win may come off as calculated self-promotion. On the phone, you won't know how the person you're talking to is reacting to the information. Your message may engender eye-rolling on the other end. When you promote in person you can read body language, observe nonverbal clues, and back off if your audience isn't receptive to your message.

Teach as You Have Been Taught

Even if you're not a sales manager, helping others is the right thing to do—for you, for your career, for your organization, and for your clients. The costs are low, yet the return can be high. Your only costs are your time and your experiences, yet your yield can be another successful salesperson on your team and a friend for life. Down the line, that friendship may

 Tackle Box

TIPS FOR BEING A GOOD CREW MEMBER

- **Never blame others for bad deals.** People know when they messed up; it's not your role to place blame. It's your role to help solve problems.

- **Everyone makes mistakes; you will too.** Help others grow from their mistakes. Offer guidance through examples.

- **Don't let others take the blame.** If you sold a bad deal or are on a team that blew a sale, then take the blame; don't let others take it for you. The fault may not be yours alone, but if you were involved, you share responsibility.

- **Don't whine or complain.** These days, anyone who's successful is overworked, tired, and bothered. So if you are too, join the club, and keep mum about it. People want to be around energetic, vigorous, outgoing people, not tired, overworked, jet-lagged individuals who complain. You don't need to be overly animated; be yourself. Just make sure that self keeps a positive outlook.

THIS AIN'T NO FISH TALE!

Many people have helped me at different junctures in my career. One great coach was my first sales manager. He embodied the fisherman's code, even though he may never have baited a hook. Many mornings he'd stroll by my desk and pose three questions: "What did you learn from your customers yesterday? What was your biggest takeaway? What did you do on the job to help someone else?" If I were slow to answer, he'd fill the space by explaining what he'd learned. He'd share tips that helped him position a product better or deepen his relationship with the prospect, or others on the team. His philosophy was that one could always learn something new. He scheduled staff meetings to discuss our deals and ways to help each other move them along. "When you are helping others, you're helping the team and yourself," he explained. "The more we function as a successful unit, the more value we can provide to our customers."

Working in a telesales center, we didn't meet face-to-face with our customers. Yet over time, I realized that his philosophy, which fostered harmony within our team and created an open environment of feedback and encouragement, allowed each of us to take risks and overcome fears about dealing with customers on tough issues. It also allowed us to openly discuss approaches and ask for advice without feeling that "we should know this stuff." Looking back, I now see that we were a close group with great results. Other colleagues were always trying to climb aboard our "boat" because of the professionalism we displayed and the values that guided our work. Our "crew," and this "captain" in particular, defined what it takes to succeed—in sales and in life.

well generate leads, new tips, and even career opportunities, if and when they arise.

When an individual shares time and talents and is involved with others' development, the organization will typically take notice. Your manager, sales director, or even your VP will note you as a team player who might have growth potential as a future leader in the organization.

We all like to be around people who can help us, or from whom we can learn. Hone your skills with your peers, and you'll improve how you conduct yourself and interact with your clients. As a sales rep, your job is to educate people about the benefits of your products and offers. Working with your peers allows you to polish your people skills. As you become less of a "salesperson" and more of a leader or expert in your field, your clients will stop thinking of you as someone who's trying to sell them something, and, instead, see you as a partner who has their best interests in mind.

Things you should strive for and impart to others:

- Honest feedback
- Accountability
- Wisdom
- Experiences
- Constructive criticism
- Compassion and understanding

Back on the Dock

Tarpon Willie tells a great story about his wife's grandfather, Hans—a strong man with an equally strong personality. Hans hailed from Holland and was stubborn as an ox, but was a big believer in honesty, discipline, and helping others. Hans owned a home on the Indian River on the east coast of Florida that he shared with his wife and two sons.

One day, he told the young boys about a big fish down on the bank that he had his eye on for two days. He suggested they throw a line in and hold on for dear life. Skeptical, the two boys asked why he hadn't caught it himself. Hans explained that he had caught many fish over his lifetime but this fish was too big for him. He was hoping one of his young, strong sons could reel it in. He went on to explain that the fish would disappear from time to time but would always return to the same spot. "Watch and listen for the fish," Hans told his sons. "When it's feeding on the smaller fish, you can track it and figure out what type of fish it is and what times of day it might bite. I've found the fish. Now you boys need to go catch it."

The boys chuckled, thinking their father had worked too hard and was suffering from heat exhaustion. They chuckled even louder when he grabbed a live chicken out of the barn and stuck it on a fishing hook that was ten times bigger than any hook they'd ever seen. They continued to chuckle as their father threw the chicken and monster hook out in the water at dusk. Their chuckles grew into belly laughs when Hans tied a chain to the hook and connected it to his tractor.

The next morning at breakfast, Hans glanced out the window and what he saw caused him to spill his coffee. Jumping up, he ran outside toward his tractor. Following him, the boys saw a major commotion in the water. Something HUGE was on the line. Hans jumped on the tractor, started it up, and yelled, "I think we got a big one!" At that, he put the tractor in gear and pulled a 900-pound Goliath grouper out of the river.

To this day, people in Stuart, Florida, still talk about that monster fish. Yet, no one ever heard Hans brag or discuss it. Everyone who witnessed the event—and the fish—tells the story. Over the years, Hans shared his secret spot with many of his friends and family. It has produced bounty for generations, but no one has ever caught another fish to match Hans's Goliath. Hans's family to this day talks about his business acumen, his fishing ability, and his generosity. He was a terrific fisherman and a good person. He knew how to spot fish, track them, catch them, and help others. Most important, he never bragged about his catch. He let others do it for him.

As you conclude this book, I hope you've enjoyed its lessons and stories and taken some to heart. I truly believe if you apply the wisdom of Tarpon Willie and all seasoned fishermen to your sales process, you too can catch the "Goliath" that's lurking just below the surface—whether it's one super sale, or a successful career. I challenge you, as I have been challenged by many excellent mentors, family members, and friends, to discipline yourself each day. Take initiative and be proactive in your quest for opportunities. As Tarpon Willie says, "If you don't get out on that boat early and put those lines in the water, you won't ever catch a fish."

May your lines always be tight!

—*Joe DiMisa*

Glossary

The following terms are some of the ones that every salesperson should understand to make sure you "talk the talk."

Accelerating Commission Plan is a plan that gives incentive to a sales rep for continued performance. The more a rep performs during a specified time, the more commissions or incentive he or she can earn. In a true accelerating commission plan, increased performance will result in increased percentages or payouts. For example, a rep who performs at 80 percent of quota might earn 50 cents for every dollar of revenue, whereas a rep who performs at 100 percent might earn 70 cents for every dollar of revenue.

Acquisition Revenue is revenue from sales to new accounts. Acquisition revenue implies targeting and acquiring new accounts and successfully selling them any product.

Billed Revenue is revenue from a product or service that has been sold and installed and for which the customer has paid. Many companies pay their reps based on billed revenue. For companies, billed revenue is fiscally responsible because no reward is paid out until the customer pays. However, this method presents a downside for sales reps because they don't get paid for the sale right away; therefore, no "clear line of sight" exists from the date of the deal to the payout for the rep.

Booked Revenue (aka Bookings) is actual revenue that is officially booked and realized during the course of the fiscal year based upon the company's accounting practices. For example, if a rep sells a five-year contract for $5 million, the company can only realize a percentage of that revenue each year. Companies must follow actual rules and contracts to realize the revenue on their financial statements. Some companies pay commissions based on booked revenues only for the year.

Breakage (aka Overallocation) is an amount or percentage added to the overall sales goal to account for underperformance in some areas. Breakage is factored into quota setting. For example, if the district sales goal is $1 million for ten reps, a breakage percentage of 10 may be factored into the quotas, giving each of the ten reps a quota of $110,000. When rolled up, the overall district quota becomes $1.1 million.

Chargebacks are a mechanism companies employ to take back crediting or rep commissions if sales don't come to fruition. In some cases, chargebacks are subtracted from the rep's next commission check; in other cases, the rep's new commissionable revenue is reduced, thereby reducing the future commission. The typical chargeback period is 90 to 180 days after the sale. Companies often use a sliding scale, based on time from sale, to determine how much of the commission or crediting must be paid back. For example, within 90 days the full amount may have to be paid back; closer to 180 days, the chargeback may be reduced to 20 percent.

Churn represents revenue, customers, and/or products that are lost over time; for instance, a rep had ten customers last year, but this year one went bankrupt, so only nine remain. The missing customer is the rep's churn. Churn can be calculated in absolute numbers or in percentages. The opposite of churn is retention, so in the example given, the rep retains nine out of the original ten customers. A high level of churn places a tough burden on a rep who must grow the business and also make up for the lost customers.

Commissionable Revenue is generated revenue that can be applied to the commission calculation. Commissionable revenue can be booked revenue, sales revenue, or billed revenue, depending on the terms of the sales commission plan. To determine a rep's commission, the commission rate is applied to the commissionable revenue. Commission rates may accelerate or decelerate based on various targets or levels of commissionable revenue.

Conversion Revenue represents additional sales to current accounts. The added sales represent revenue growth, typically through adding new products into the mix of products bought by the account. Conversion requires a focus on aggressively capturing more revenue from current relationships.

Compensation Cost of Sales (CCOS) is the actual cost of all the base salary and incentive paid to a sales rep. This measure is typically used at an aggregate level (all salespeople) to determine how much an organization is paying in total sales expense. It does not include support costs or employee benefit expenses.

Draw is a commission payment paid out prior to a sale being made. Draws are typically used for new reps or reps who have long selling cycles and face cash-flow issues. Two types of draws are used. In a *recoverable* draw, the company can get the draw back if the rep doesn't sell up to requirements. Recoverable draws are used for sales reps with tenure. A *nonrecoverable* draw typically is given to new reps for a period of time to help them get on board. Companies typically do not get nonrecoverable draws back.

Excellence Points describe the levels of attainment a rep has to achieve in order to earn accelerated commission dollars. Excellence points are typically set based upon historic performance of the top 10 percent of an organization.

Funnel (aka Pipeline) describes the total amount of potential revenue from identified and/or qualified sales opportunities. The term "funnel" is used more often than is "pipeline," but "pipeline" refers to the total amount of potential, whereas "funnel" has stages of qualifications. *Above funnel* indicates all the activities a rep is doing to generate excitement. Depending on the business, this could include cold calling, industry networking, writing articles, giving speeches, sending out mailings, and entertaining potential customers—all above-funnel work. When these activities create awareness and the rep is able to qualify opportunities, those opportunities are counted in the funnel. Sales are the output of the funnel.

Forecast (aka Yield—Pipeline Yield or Funnel Yield) represents the amount of deals in the funnel or pipeline that are estimated to close and result in actual revenue. Within the pipeline are identi-fied opportunities, qualified opportunities, proposed opportuni-ties, and closed opportunities. Each of these may have different odds of actually closing. For example, only 10 percent of identi-fied opportunities may close; 20 percent of qualified opportuni-ties; 50% of proposed opportunities, and so on. The forecast is the total potential revenue of each opportunity multiplied by its potential to close. So the pipeline may hold $100,000, but the combined forecast is 30 percent of that, or $30,000.

Margin is a term used to describe the spread between cost of your product or service and the price at which you can sell it. In world-class organizations, margin is tracked regularly.

Overlay is used to describe a sales specialist or subject matter expert (SME) who is used within a sales force to provide expertise in a specific area; examples are network, data, or product special-ists. These individuals typically do not own a set of accounts but work in conjunction with a rep who has ownership of an account. They have a specific area of expertise and focus only on that area.

Pareto Analysis involves calculating the relative importance and concentration of revenue sources. For example, 20 percent of the sales reps account for 80 percent of revenue, or the top five customer accounts bring in 60 percent of revenue. Pareto analy-sis is useful in identifying which factors have the most impact on a business and where a business should focus its efforts. Other types of Pareto analyses may determine revenue per employee versus compensation cost per employee, existing revenue versus potential revenue, and so on.

Pay/Performance Analysis measures the correlation between a performance measure and a pay component and estimates what the average pay should be for a given level of performance. The correlation value ranges from 0 to 1. Correlation values below .75 suggest no strong relationship between pay and performance; correlation values above .75 indicate that the given performance measure is a very good indicator of how much pay is received.

Retention Revenue is current revenue maintained in current accounts. By definition, retention percentages cannot exceed

100 percent of sales to the account in the prior year. Any increase in revenue to current accounts is considered to be conversion revenue. If less than 100 percent of prior revenue is retained, the lost amount is referred to as churn (see earlier definition).

Sales Revenue is the anticipated revenue for the total deal. Sales revenue is typically considered a proxy for billed revenue. When calculating sales revenue, the company uses a formula to account for churn (see earlier definition), reducing the actual sales price by a percentage. For example, say the total deal is $60,000, with $5,000 to be billed each month for twelve months. The company expects a 10 percent churn, so the actual sales revenue is set at $54,000, or $4,500 per month. Using sales revenue as the basis for commissions is preferred by reps because it provides clear line of sight plus immediate gratification, as reps receive immediate credit for the sale. For the company, it presents the dilemma of paying commissions before the revenue comes in.

Threshold is the minimum acceptable level of sales or revenue that earns a rep commission or incentive. Performance below threshold typically means a lower, or even no, commission or incentive. At threshold, a rep will typically earn the minimum. Once sales reach the threshold target, the rep then earns a percentage of his or her target incentive or commission.

Trend (aka Sales Trend, Deal Trend, or Revenue Trend) involves looking at past performance and trying to predict where the company, district, or rep is headed in terms of sales. For example, if $50,000 is sold in January, $70,000 in February, and $90,000 in March, the trend is $110,000 in April.

Variable Cost of Sales (VCOS) is the actual cost of all the incentive paid to a sales rep. This measure is typically used at an aggregate level (all salespeople) to determine how much an organization is paying in variable sales expense. It does not include support cost or employee benefit expenses.

Yield is the anticipated closed sales or revenue from the sales pipeline once all of the individual deal probabilities have been factored in. The yield is commonly used in forecasting the end of the month, quarter, or year.

Index

About the Author

JOE DIMISA has fifteen years of experience in direct sales, marketing management, training, operations, compensation and quota setting, strategy planning, and telephone sales. He has consulted with startup and large organizations, including AT&T, BellSouth, Cisco Systems, Equifax, Business Objects, and Verizon. DiMisa is currently head of the Sales and Marketing Practice at Sibson Consulting, a division of the Segal Company. He resides in Tampa, FL.